M000168810

Holy Bible, Human Bible

Using the Bible in Pastoral Practice

Series Editors: Stephen Pattison and David Spriggs

Titles in the series:

The Bible in Pastoral Practice: Readings in the Place and Function of Scripture in the Church
Edited by Paul Ballard and Stephen R. Holmes

Holy Bible, Human Bible: Questions Pastoral Practice Must Ask
Gordon Oliver

Holy Bible, Human Bible

Questions Pastoral Practice Must Ask

Gordon Oliver

WILLIAM B. EERDMANS PUBLISHING COMPANY
GRAND RAPIDS, MICHIGAN / CAMBRIDGE, U.K.

First published 2006
in the United Kingdom by
Darton, Longman and Todd Ltd
1 Spencer Court, 140–142 Wandsworth High Street
London, SW18 4JJ
and in the United States of America by
Wm. B. Eerdmans Publishing Co.
2140 Oak Industrial Drive N.E., Grand Rapids, Michigan 49505 /
P.O. Box 163, Cambridge CB3 9PU U.K.
www.eerdmans.com

Printed in the United States of America

10 09 08 07 06   7 6 5 4 3 2 1

ISBN-10 0-8028-3201-6
ISBN-13 978-0-8028-3201-6

Designed by Sandie Boccacci

To Ros, Jonathan and Anna

Contents

Series Preface

The book you have before you is part of a three-volume series on using the Bible in pastoral practice.

The series is the fruit of a partnership between Bible Society and the School of Religious and Theological Studies at Cardiff University. Bible Society wants to make the voice of the Bible heard everywhere; this project aims to develop critical awareness of the ways in which the Bible is, and might better be, used in pastoral practice.

We take pastoral practice to be the activity of Christians that nurtures flourishing in all areas of human life – individual, ecclesiastical and social. So it might include campaigning against world debt, managing health-care organisations, chairing congregational meetings, preaching, taking school assemblies, neighbourhood visiting, bereavement counselling and conducting weddings, amongst many other activities. Pastoral practice thus widely defined includes the activities of lay people and clergy.

The project group's working assumption is that the Bible pertains, or should pertain, directly and indirectly to all pastoral activities. However, there seems to be little specific knowledge of how the Bible is actually used, or systematic consideration as to how it might be used better. So one of our aims has been actually to document the ways in which the Bible is and might be used.

A summary report of this preliminary empirical investigation, carried out by a specially appointed Fellow of the University, can be found on the School of Religious Studies website at Cardiff University (www.cardiff.ac.uk). This has been supplemented by historical and theoretical explorations in the practical interpretation of the Bible. One outcome of the project is the production of three books which, severally and together, should enable those involved in pastoral practice to analyse their own present use of the Bible and to learn how to use it more creatively.

The first of the books, *The Bible in Practice*, provides a rich overview of the ways in which Christians have, and could, use the Bible in their pastoral work. In the present volume, *Holy Bible, Human Bible*, Gordon

Oliver, an experienced pastor and theologian, presents a personal view of the way in which the Bible challenges pastoral practice and pastoral practice challenges understandings of the Bible. Oliver has drawn on his own experience and extensive research to produce a lively and controversial text that should stimulate readers to reconsider the ways in which they think about and use the world's 'greatest unread book'. The final book, *Using the Bible in Christian Ministry: A Workbook*, draws upon the empirical research and the other two books to enable pastoral workers to audit, analyse and improve their daily practice. It thus earths the whole series in everyday pastoral reality and makes the series not just intellectually stimulating but also directly useful.

As series editors, we are grateful to the editors, authors and contributors to all the books and to our publishers. If this volume and its companions succeed in opening up more critical and creative opportunities for the Bible in pastoral practice at all levels, then all the work that has been done will have been well worth while.

David Spriggs, *Bible Society*
Stephen Pattison, *Cardiff University*
Series Editors

Foreword

I firmly believe in using the Bible in our pastoral practice. I have done so over the years and found it to be healing and beneficial in people's lives. But with time some of my earlier naïvety has inevitably been tempered. Merely quoting proof texts at people in the hope that it will settle issues and provide unquestionable guidance is problematic for a number of reasons. Which texts do we quote? Some appear to contradict others, so how do we select? Do the texts really apply? After all, the Bible was written in very different cultures from our own, centuries ago. Are we sure that the words carry the contemporary weight we wish to give them? How will the texts be heard? To me the Bible has always been a positive and liberating book. However others have only ever heard it as a voice of authority, repression and even violence. Do we abuse the text when quoting a bit out of context? We all know how journalists can make it appear that politicians have said the opposite of what they actually said by isolating their words. Are we in danger of doing that with the Bible? How can the Bible be true, or even contain truth, for a generation that is unsure of the existence of truth?

These and others are the questions Gordon Oliver addresses with honesty and skill in this enjoyable book. Although well-grounded in theological understanding, from the very first chapter the book is written about the typical situations pastors face. He introduces us to a variety of real life situations where the Bible is read, interpreted and applied – real life situations that expose the contradictoriness and messiness of people's reading of the Bible. The people we meet at the start keep returning in later chapters and are joined by others as Gordon illustrates, applies and tests his arguments against them.

Significant chapters unpack a variety of crucial issues such as the relationship between contemporary pastoral practice with, for example, its non-judgemental approach and agenda of self-fulfilment and the gospel witness to Jesus; the way in which the Bible can open gates that separate people and build bridges between them or be used to draw boundaries; and the place of the Bible in the church, the role of 'authority' figures in the community and the question of tolerance. He ends by exploring the challenging question, 'Can we be human and biblical at the same time?'

If readers want to find a simple technique, a step-by-step pragmatic approach to using the Bible pastorally, they will not find it here. But they will be led to face up to the hard questions that come from all angles – from the angle of those who doubt the Bible can be used at all, as much as from the angle of those who would use it glibly – and they will be led by a wise guide towards working out for themselves approaches and perspectives that are richer and more viable than their starting point.

Gordon Oliver obviously had a background similar to my own. He entered ministry with an absolute certainty about the Bible and its role. But then he discovered that 'not very many of the people [he] worked with knew the questions that fitted the answers' he was ready to give. He has resolved that dilemma at times in ways that are different from the solutions I have come to. That means I differ on occasions from the directions he takes in this book. But it made me reflect on my own approach. I found every part of the book thought-provoking and enriching of my own pastoral use of the Bible.

I certainly want to affirm the vision of being biblical that is expounded here. Gordon writes:

> Being biblical does not mean turning occasionally to the Bible for help when we meet a puzzling pastoral situation. That would be like family members only speaking to each other when they want something to be handed over, but otherwise living in estrangement under the same roof. To be biblical is to live in a continuing, comfortable, and argumentative relationship with the Bible. It means living in the *oikonomia*, the household, where the speaking of God is expected to be experienced as part of everyday normality. The habit of listening to the Bible, speaking its words, singing its songs, dwelling on its pictures, reflecting on its teachings, allowing its messages to grate and bore as well as to comfort and stimulate, is the essential context for discovering what it means to include the speaking of God in pastoral practice. This makes for mature adult relationships with the Bible rather than childish ones which as we grow up have to be put away (1 Corinthians 13:11).

The introduction endorses the importance of 'charitable listening' as a way of working through disagreements and confusions and as a sign of loving our neighbours as we love ourselves. I hope pastors of all complexions will engages in active and charitable listening to what is written within this book in order that the Bible may find again a credible, constructive and liberating voice in our pastoral practice.

Derek Tidball
London School of Theology

Introduction: Come and See

This book explores questions about the Bible that ordinary Christians would like to ask if only they could get the chance. People who are beginning their ministry and theological studies as well as more experienced pastoral practitioners and Bible teachers will find it especially helpful. It asks a lot of questions in ways that I hope are fresh, well-grounded and open-ended. Curiosity and questions are essential starting points for Christian growing and Christian learning. Major killers of creative engagement with Scripture include lack of imagination, lack of curiosity, and constricted approaches to practical Christian living. The most important questions are the ones we don't yet know the answers to, not the ones that are set up to give clever people platforms to say what they already know everybody else should think.

Since for Christians the Bible is the Word of God in human words you would expect it to connect the speaking of God, the concerns of the people who wrote it, and the concerns of God's people today. This is exactly what happens. The Bible is human as well as holy and this simple fact raises lots of questions about what kind of a thing the Bible really is and how the Word of God and the words of Scripture relate to each other. If the Bible as the Word of God only delivered the sound of one voice speaking – the voice of God – everything would be simple, at least in principle. Every word of Scripture would carry the authority of God's will and you would be faced with the simple choice of going along with what it says or taking the risk of staying outside of God's will.

But it's not like that at all because the Bible contains the speaking of many voices. It presents the testimonies of hundreds of different people speaking about their experiences of God's guidance, inspiration, warnings, comfort and so on. On top of that individual texts carry multiple layers of meaning according to how you understand them in their original contexts, and who you are and where you are when you read them. The same text can carry different messages for different people. Jesus' reading of Isaiah in Luke 4:16–18 could serve as a general challenge to the social conscience of a settled suburban congregation; or as a message of reassurance to people suffering from social exclusion by powerful others; or to legitimate commitment to direct political action by social activists; or as an interpretive key to be used by New Testament scholars who understand the ministry of Jesus as prophetic teaching about the coming of God's kingdom. When a single text can speak in so many ways you have to ask whose understanding of the text is the right one, or whether they are all the right one, but for different people. If there is disagreement about this, whose understanding should take priority? In other words, who owns the Bible?

Even in these times of almost universal literacy in the Western world, when nearly everybody who wants to can have their own Bible, most Christians, most of the time, hear the words of Scripture, sing them as hymns and songs and pray them in church much more often than they encounter them as text to be read. This means that how you *hear* the Bible matters. Churches in the West are often linked to attitudes of conservatism and conformity, so the hearing, singing and praying of Scripture tends to domesticate the Bible, depriving it of its essential oddness and wildness and reinforcing the idea that Jesus is a Christian rather like us, but better. This kind of conformity can also serve to deprive God of his rightful freedom of speech because the Word of God gets masked behind the word of the church. This is why it is important to ask how the Bible really witnesses to Jesus Christ and helps people, in the words of Philip Yancey, to 'meet Jesus again for the first time'.

A major purpose of Christian pastoral practice is to embody and put into action the values of the gospel of Christ, particularly through promoting the growth of persons and communities. Pastoral practice is one of the major ways in which Christians promote the mission of God in the world. At the centre of this mission is Jesus Christ: his teaching, his actions, his dying, his aliveness. But Christian pastoral practice becomes increasingly specialised through its focus on particular commitments such as counselling, social action and therapy. Moreover, it is lived out in a society that is full of pastoral practice carried out through schools, health centres, rehabilitation units, probation services, child protection services, care of the elderly, etc. This means that pastoral practice and the care of people is increasingly regulated and Christians have to give attention to this as much as anybody else, so it is inevitable that pastoral practice must ask the Bible another set of questions. How far does Jesus in particular and the

Bible more generally support or challenge the values of secular and externally regulated pastoral practice?

Christians at the start of the twenty-first century have to face up to some challenges to their belief and practice that were already on the agenda when the Bible was being written, including the relationship between rich and poor, respect for creation, relationships between women and men, same gender relationships, right use and ownership of land, etc. Other issues that were not even thought of until quite recently must also be considered, such as the opportunities presented by genetic research, fertility treatments and the like. These are all issues that Christians disagree about, often bitterly accusing people who don't see the truth as they see it of being unbiblical, or even no kind of Christians at all. Truth claims are very often also power claims, and 'biblical' Christians may claim a monopoly on biblical truth as their power base for insisting that Christians who see issues differently should be kept at a distance or even rejected altogether. This means that hard questions have to be asked about what role the Bible could play in setting boundaries or forming bridges between believers who deeply disagree with one another. Where does the Bible really belong in relation to the local church, and how can a congregation's engagement with Scripture be made more realistic, more faith-building, more fruitful?

In Christian history the Bible has been used to dehumanise people, as it has been appealed to in order to justify the subjugation of women by men; the separation of poor people from the wealthy; slavery; apartheid, radical separation from unbelievers and much else besides. This darker side of the history of the use of the Bible provokes perhaps the most important question of all: can we be biblical and human at the same time? Wherever God first meets the people he loves, he calls them to become as fully human as he created all humanity to be. The Bible describes this as being called to 'grow to maturity, to the full measure of the stature of Christ' (Ephesians 4:13). The question is how the Bible can become a truly open book for Christians; how can the voices both of Scripture and of present-day Christians have genuine freedom of speech? This freedom to talk realistically and faithfully with God and the people of God is a major foundation for the liberation and transformation of people that forms the purpose and the bedrock of both truly Christian engagement with Scripture and Christian pastoral practice.

I come to these questions as a pastor, teacher and practical theologian. When I was first ordained I knew absolutely what the Bible was for. It was to be proclaimed 'in season and out of season' with confidence and conviction. The answers to all of life's questions could be found there. My job was to know the answers and teach them. As a rather fundamentalist evangelical I knew a lot of these answers. Unfortunately, not very many of the people I worked with knew the questions that fitted the answers. At theological seminary we were told that Jesus meets people where they are, but where the people I met were was often in a terrible mess and, truth to tell, this was sometimes true of me as well. The straightforward answers I had learned did not always work. In fact they didn't often work. It was time to grow up and learn new ways of being human, Christian and evangelical all at the same time.

This has been quite a journey. I remain convinced of God's love and God's calling in Jesus Christ for all people. In my journey I soon discovered two gifts that I have found essential to my spirituality and ministry. These are sheer uselessness and insatiable curiosity. I used to envy pastors who could do clever things like play musical instruments, enjoy electronic devices, fix things in the church building, or be interested in the finer points of liturgy or history. Then it dawned on me that because I could do none of these there would be plenty of room for other people to do them. The only gift I really needed to bring was space for people and God to speak and work together. Insatiable curiosity is wonderful because it keeps you asking questions and wondering why things are the way they are and how they might get to be different and better. Curiosity means that for as long as I have been a pastor I have been a learner, and I have reckoned that the people I work with in churches and other settings are my teachers. It is wonderful to have so many of them!

Two things that make learning and growing as God's people possible are hospitality and generosity of spirit. Among Christians who put questions to the Bible and disagree about the answers that they find, these qualities have never been more needed than they are now. I find Stephen Fowl's teaching in *Engaging Scripture* about the priority of 'charitable listening' particularly helpful here, because it involves listening carefully to what the other person is saying and putting the best possible interpretation on it. This opens up the opportunity for some of the sharpest disagreements and confusions to be worked through by people who are committed to the welfare of one another – that is, to loving their neighbours as themselves. When Christians apply these principles to the ways they hear and read the Bible, the way is opened for the Word of God to dwell among us, 'full of grace and truth'. When this happens there can be no escape into the detached fantasy and romanticism that take the guts out of Christian spirituality. Pastoral practice must ask hard questions of the Bible in the sure knowledge that the Bible will ask hard questions back. In this way the gates can be opened for the Bible, pastoral practice and Christian mission to travel riskily along the same road.

Acknowledgements

My gratitude goes to all members of the Bible in Pastoral Practice Steering Group, especially to Professor Stephen Pattison and Professor Paul Ballard of Cardiff University and Dr David Spriggs of the Bible Society, who have inspired, provoked and encouraged me throughout the writing. Thanks also to Anne, Chris, Jean, Theresa and all my colleagues in the Ministry and Training Department in Rochester Diocese for their support, encouragement and patience. Above all, my love and thanks to my family, who have helped me to stay a learner and have taught me more about the speaking of God and the love of God than they will ever know.

Gordon Oliver
Rochester
July 2005

CHAPTER 1

What Is a Bible?

Surprises

Christians call the Bible 'the Word of God'. They hear such clear echoes between the Bible and their experience that time itself seems to be bypassed as God's truth becomes present, attractive, demanding. There are two surprises about this. First that this book, written between two and three thousand years ago in contexts of languages and cultures as far removed from twenty-first century Britain and America as you could imagine, is still in regular use. The Bible is a more 'open book' than ever. The complete text has been translated into around 400 languages, and sections of it into a huge number of languages and local dialects. People sing its words in worship, pray its prayers and seek inspiration, guidance, challenge, comfort and spiritual renewal through what they find in it. It is not surprising that in a world where everything is changing all the time people want a 'word' they can trust. What is surprising is that they find it here and that they call it 'the word of the Lord'.

The second surprise is that many Christians appear not to be surprised at all by what they read in the Bible. This is probably due to the association of the Bible with the Church. For centuries in the West 'church' has been almost synonymous in the popular imagination with cultural conformity and conservatism. This means the Bible is read with the expectation that it will support the cultural ways of being Christian that the churches commend. But the Scriptures are much more like a caged animal, restless to be set free to disrupt and challenge the assumptions of its hearers and readers, than like a pet animal that has become a kind of lifestyle accessory for Christians who happen to value it. To press the illustration, when it became caged the restless animal lost its ability to communicate. When it is set free a transformation occurs. This 'animal' can talk after all. When the Bible talks, and you get used to its languages and accents, you begin to recognise the disturbing, attracting speaking of God.

When we consider what the Bible is and the kinds of questions pastoral practice makes us ask about it, wild and disruptive responses of honesty and openness and of wilful or accidental suppression are never far away. For example, it is commonplace among Christians in Britain and the United States to assume that academic biblical scholars are living in one interpretive world and that preachers and congregations are living in another. During their seminary training pastors commonly encounter huge difficulties in holding together the outcomes of critical biblical scholarship and their own faith commitment to treating the Bible as the word of God. The standard way of resolving this issue is to decide in favour of the 'faith option' rather than the 'scholarship option' and to leave congregations in ignorance of the questions raised by biblical scholarship. The assumption of such pastors is that congregations would be likely to find issues raised by historical criticism too complicated and disturbing. There may be some truth in this, though I think there is at least an element of the pastors projecting their own fears too. What is clear, however, is that the implications for how congregations relate to the Bible are enormous. Before we explore these issues, we will visit some ordinary Christians who are trying to make sense of what the Bible is for themselves.

Quiet Time

A teenager lies on the floor in front of the TV. Scattered around are videos, homework books and a packet of sweets. The soap she is half-watching shows teens struggling with their parents, their love life, their ambitions. She has her Bible open and is poring over a passage in Matthew – something about serving God and mammon. She looks from the Bible to the screen and then to her Bible reading notes. She scribbles something in the margin of her Bible. She prays at the end of her 'quiet time'. We might think she would be better off trying to pray in a quieter place, and that would probably be true. But here is a young woman using the Bible, seeking to discern God's voice speaking through Scripture among the many other voices around her. Texts between two and three thousand years old are being used in a twenty-first century room in front of the TV. The expectation is that as God spoke in ancient times God can speak his word through the Scriptures now. This seeking to hear God's voice in Scripture as one among the many other voices speaking about values, lifestyles and vocations has become a completely normal part of spirituality for many Christians.

'This Is the Gospel of Christ'

In the cathedral the organ blasts out a fanfare as the deacon, holding the Gospel Book high above her head, is led in procession by cross-bearer and acolytes up to the middle of the aisle. As the Gospel is announced and incense billows upwards everybody turns to face the reader. She reads the passage from Luke about how much more difficult it is for a rich man to enter the kingdom of God than for a camel to get through the eye of a needle. At the end of the reading she holds the book aloft crying out, 'This is the Gospel of Christ' and the choir bursts into song, 'Praise to Christ our Lord'. Here are ancient texts being read in a deeply-rooted historical context and held up as nothing less than the words of Jesus Christ himself spoken today.

Home Group

David was made redundant by the company where he worked for 25 years. He misses the routine of going to work, his friends and col-leagues. He feels out of place at home all day. He doesn't know what to do with himself. The loneliness and pointlessness are crushing him. Nobody seems to have anything useful to say. His pastor gives him odd jobs to do around the church, but doesn't really seem to listen to him. In his home group David hears somebody reading from Psalm 139: 'O Lord, you have searched me and known me, you know when I sit down and when I rise up; you discern my thoughts from far away . . .' The passage rings bells for him and he begins to share his feelings with the other members of the group. His new openness enables others to share from their experience. Here a group of friends discover that an ancient prayer from the Bible can become their prayer too. It resonates with their experience and opens the way for them to share what really matters to them. Ancient Scripture has become literally a word of life now.

Biblical Christians?

Ian has been vicar of St Peter's for five years. The congregation have responded warmly to his style of preaching and many people have transferred into St Peter's from other parishes. Ian is regarded as a leader of evangelical opinion in the area. He is dismayed by what he regards as the liberal line taken by the Bishop on gay issues and goes to challenge him about the matter. The Bishop listens as Ian expounds the biblical teaching from Leviticus and Romans about homosexual-ity, then tries to take the conversation forward by suggesting that a more open engagement with Bible texts might be helpful. He offers texts about welcoming strangers and treating them with hospitality and respect and commends a more theological than textual approach to the interpretation of Scripture. At the end they agree to talk again about these things, but privately both of them believe that the other one is not really a biblical Christian. Here are people engaging with a present-day pastoral and ethical issue. Both seek to root their position in Scripture, but both take quite different approaches to understanding the status of texts as the basis of guidance about moral living.

Community Protest

The residents of a small town are up in arms because the government plans to build an international airport that will mean the demolition of most of their homes and businesses and environmental destruction on a grand scale. When they understand the size of investment by building companies that will be involved, they feel powerless and depressed. However some residents decide to form an action group to plan a protest campaign. Churches encourage their members to join in, and organise prayer and Bible study groups to consider the issues. These groups draw encouragement from their reflections about God's justice being worked out by and through vulnerable people.

One day Geoff tells the members of his Bible study group that he has been talking with two of his neighbours about the airport plans. One of them is a Sikh and the other a Muslim. They had said they had been discussing at the Gudwarah and at the Mosque how they could learn from their Scriptures to respond to the proposals. Here we have Christians seeking guidance in the Bible to help them play their part in responding to an urgent social and political issue. But other faith groups in the same place are doing the same thing – more than one 'Bible' is involved. As they try to identify scriptural foundations for their protest, Geoff and his home group may ask themselves what is distinctive about the *Christian* Scriptures.

New Testament Class

Susan is a New Testament tutor in a seminary. She wants her students to explore the issues involved in interpreting the themes of law and grace in the letters of Paul. She tries to open a discussion on whether you can read the Letter to the Romans without considering how Protestant theological thinking in the twenty-first century about law and grace has been influenced by the theology and politics of the sixteenth-century Reformation. She is frustrated in this because her students think the contrast between law (= negative) and grace (= positive) is completely clear, and they just want to get on and 'preach the good news'.

Experience First

In five of these six stories concerns about the context, authorship, original purpose and history of interpretation of biblical texts are invisible or well in the background. The main criterion for Scripture interpretation here is directly reflected experience. In technical terms, the hermeneutical method is one of parallel correlation. The present experience of the Bible reader and the text of Scripture are held together in parallel and the correlations and dissonances between them constitute the learning that becomes available. The proposed encounter with the Scriptures is immediate. The interpretation arises directly from the concerns and the spirituality of the people involved. The academic world of textual analysis, critical studies, history of interpretation and other disciplines of biblical studies is simply not relevant. The Bible has leap-frogged from its origins in the past straight into the present and is available for immediate interpretation. The tools for interpretation consist of the experiences and questions of the Scripture readers. And, as we might say, since God, being eternally present, is our contemporary, we experience here and now the presence of the Holy Spirit to enlighten and guide us in the ways of Jesus Christ as we read the Scriptures that witness to him.

This way of engaging with Scripture has some important advantages as well as some obvious limitations. The main advantage is that provided the people concerned are committed to seeking God's will and to hearing what God might want to say; and provided that they have good readable translations of the Bible, anybody can do it. You just say a prayer and get on with it. You discover what God has to say and consider what kind of action is needed by way of response. There is the possibility that the word of God will truly prove to be 'living and active'. At its best this approach can lead to a refreshing encounter with Scripture that opens up new resources for practical Christian living.

The limitations include the strong possibility that personal agendas or unspoken norms of group behaviour will lead to favoured passages of Scripture being used often, while other more challenging texts are ignored. In effect, Scripture takes on the role of a mirror in which the readers discern their own reflections disguised as God's guidance, rather than of an open window though which God's voice is calling them to come outside and join him. This limitation is compounded when we consider the fact that many Christian groups are gatherings of culturally like-minded people who have an unspoken agreement not to challenge each other's views. The concern is to respect each person present as an individual so each person's contribution has to be affirmed as equally valid. This can lead to a well-mannered pooling of ignorance rather than to genuine growth in the knowledge and love of God. Although the purpose is that Scripture will speak with freshness and directness, in effect the 'animal' becomes domesticated as interpretations become increasingly conventional and less likely to challenge community norms.

I have said that in these pictures the fruits of biblical scholarship are invisible or even regarded as irrelevant. They are unlikely, however to be completely absent. For example, the writer of the Bible study notes used by the teenager will have engaged in critical biblical study. The cathedral congregation cannot but be aware of the historical feel of their environment – it has a substantial role in bringing them together. Ian and his Bishop will have read their Bible commentaries and studied the Scripture texts with care. The spiritual leaders supporting the people affected by the airport development will have studied their Scriptures and considered issues of interpreting them. But we are still forced to the conclusion that the major engagement with the text of the Bible for Christians today, like most of their forebears, can be described as 'pre-critical' rather than 'critically aware'.

It is important at this point to notice that the expression 'pre-critical' in relation to Scripture interpretation is commonly used in two ways, because our understanding of these distinctions affects what sort of thing we think the Bible is.

First, engaging with the Bible in a pre-critical way means reading its stories and sayings as if they are directly about now as well as about the time when they were written. It means reading the Bible often in a quite literal way, taking the text at its face value. 'Pre-critical' readers have few problems with the parts of Scripture where God is described as speaking directly to people and acting in miraculous ways. Since God is consistent and communicates clearly there is no reason why the God who spoke and acted in the Bible should not speak and act in similar ways today. This can lead to the Bible being treated as a kind of treasury of oracles and promises to be claimed by the readers, rather than as whole texts that need to be allowed to have their own distinctive voices.

Certainly, most 'pre-critical' readings will recognise the different genres of literature in the Bible, but there will be a specially strong commitment to the 'happenedness' of the sections regarded as historical. This has implications for how the Bible as a whole is read, but is especially important for how Christians understand the Old Testament. There can be a reluctance to grant a primarily theologically- or symbolically- rather than historically-driven significance to some Old Testament 'writings' such as Job, Jonah and Daniel. The prophetic books, especially Isaiah (and in particular chapter 53), are seen as directly pointing to Christ rather than being allowed primary significance for their own time. Indeed, the Old Testament gets to be seen as a Christian book that prepares the way for the coming of Christ rather than as a collection of Jewish books that has taken on new significance because of Christ. The failure to recognise as a key principle that Christian interpretation of the Old Testament often involves reading back from the New Testament to the Old Testament, rather than the other way round, leads to marginalisation, or even rejection, of the Jewish roots of the Christian faith. There is only a short step from this to unintentionally developing a kind of creeping anti-Semitism in Christian engagement with Scripture.

But there can be other pastoral and political implications too. This kind of 'pre-critical' interpretation is often coupled with highly selective readings of the text, that lead to overemphasis on one issue while others are completely ignored, without any conscious rationale as to why this happens. Two basic examples will illustrate why this may be pastorally and politically dangerous. First, the Pentateuchal law codes comment on lending money with interest just as often as they refer to homosexuality. But the call to stand against the latter is elevated in some churches to almost the level of an Article of the Faith, whilst theological critique of the former is virtually absent from Christian discourse. Second, the call to God's people in the Old Testament to visit destruction on the peoples of the land and to live separately from any that remain (e.g. Joshua 3:7–10; 8:18–29) – in twenty-first century terms, ethnic cleansing – can be read without any reference to other biblical injunctions to love neighbour and even enemy. It is easy to see how some 'pre-critical' reading of the Bible can lead to social and political exclusion going unchallenged or unreflected on by some Christian groups.

The problem with this kind of pre-critical reading of Scripture is that it puts the interests, needs, and presuppositions of the reader at the centre of the process. On some hilltops in the north of England are remains of ancient 'map-stones'. These are circular, indicating that to

see the surrounding countryside clearly you have to put yourself at
the centre of the map. Everything is seen from that point of view.
Applied to the Bible, this can lead to a consumerist way of reading the
Bible – a look at the text will confirm my opinions and do me good.

However, it is a mistake to imagine that all of the outcomes of 'pre-
critical' reading of this kind are necessarily negative. If people do take
Scripture at face value and act on it, this will have clear results for
how they live in families, deal with money, honour parents, relate to
neighbours, respond to sickness, overcome their sins and weaknesses,
face their deaths, bear witness to their faith, seek justice in the world,
and live in confidence as people saved through Christ. At its best, this
approach can issue in encounters with holy Scripture that lead to holy
living. Indeed, is better to characterise this kind of reading at its best
as 'naïve' in the technical sense: innocent, fresh, unaffected.[1]

Engagement with Scripture may be 'pre-critical' in this first sense of
the term, but if it is to be allowed as one kind of Christian engagement
it cannot claim to be *uncritical.* People encountering Scripture have
context and inheritance as well as their present circumstances and
needs. The role of the person who leads people in Bible reading will
often be to bring this context and inheritance into the open so that the
encounter with Scripture can be enriched and deepened.

The second meaning of 'pre-critical' refers to how Scripture was
interpreted before the arrival of historical critical studies with their
modernist commitment to analysis of the forms, sources, language
and editing of the text. In these earlier periods (roughly up to the
seventeenth century CE), there were many formalised ways of interpreting the Bible. These were driven by spiritual and theological
commitment. David Steinmetz[2] has explored how 'pre-critical'
engagement with Scripture was carried on for centuries using formal
rules or methods of interpretation. He highlights the 'fourfold sense
of Scripture' that was taken as a norm by the Church in the West from
the time of John Cassian (340–435 CE) to the Reformation and beyond.

1. The *literal* sense was the first and preferred means of fulfilling the
   purpose of Scripture – to call Christians to demonstrate the theological virtues of faith, hope and love. However, when the literal
   sense was insufficient, for example in relation to texts judged to be
   in some sense sub-Christian, because they commended violence,
   hatred of enemies, or eroticism, three other strategies could be
   applied.

2. The *allegorical* sense taught about the Church and what it should believe. It corresponded to the virtue of faith.
3. The *tropological* sense taught about individuals and what they should do. It corresponded to the virtue of love.
4. The *analogical* sense pointed to the future and wakened expectation. It corresponded to the virtue of hope.

In spite of the strange (to modern ears) results sometimes produced by this kind of formal system of interpretation, it would be more accurate to describe it as a kind of 'theological-critical' process rather than using the dismissive-sounding expression 'pre-critical'. In plain language this kind of interpretation is motivated by the life of faith and the mission of the Church. It is easy to forget that most of the greatest Bible interpreters from the early church until well after the Reformation were pastors, evangelists, missionaries and monks and that their work of Bible interpretation was directed to the purposes that went with those circumstances. They were people of passionate faith, deep prayer and determined witness. The theological-critical methods of reading the Bible that they used operated according to highly refined rules of evidence and interpretation, which were often the subject of vigorous dispute, as much as modern historical critical approaches. Their methods depended for their effectiveness on the Bible interpreters being rooted in the Church, but at the same time being critical of the Church and seeking its renewal.

Their purpose was to make the whole of Scripture wholly available to the whole of the Church as it did theology in the forms of worship, prayer, mission, politics, economics, art, etc. They achieved this by enabling Scripture to speak with a number of different tones and accents simultaneously as the theological virtues found their voices through the text of the Bible. One advantage of this approach was that it took seriously some of the parts of Scripture, mostly in the Old Testament, that are deeply unpalatable to Christian tastes. Steinmetz offers an entertaining example of the importance of this multi-accented approach.

> How was a French parish priest in 1150 to understand Psalm 137, which bemoans captivity in Babylon, makes rude remarks about Edomites, expresses an ineradicable longing for a glimpse of Jerusalem, and pronounces a blessing on anyone who avenges the destruction of the Temple by dashing Babylonian children against a rock? The priest lives in Concale, not Babylon, has no

personal quarrel with Edomites, cherishes no ambitions to visit Jerusalem (though he might fancy a holiday in Paris) and is expressly forbidden by Jesus to avenge himself on his enemies. Unless Psalm 137 has more than one possible meaning, it cannot be used as a prayer by the Church and must be rejected as a lament belonging exclusively to the piety of ancient Israel.[3]

Figurative or symbolic readings of Scripture have their roots within the Bible itself. For example, Paul offers typological interpretations of the Old Testament text, which he then develops in new directions to press his argument about the nature and work of Christ. Two straight-forward examples are his use of contrasting typology to discuss the resurrection of believers in 1 Corinthians 15:21–22 'as in Adam all die, even so in Christ shall all be made alive'; and his interpretation of the role of the law as 'a schoolmaster to bring us to Christ' in Galatians 3:24.[4] His allegorical use of the stories of the sons of Hagar and Sarah which we find in Galatians 4:21–26 is much more difficult to appreci-ate in the twenty-first century: 'Now Hagar is Mount Sinai in Arabia and corresponds to the present Jerusalem, for she is in slavery with her children.' I wonder whether, if Paul was writing in the twenty-first century, he would be regarded as a liberal or as an evangelical in his use of Scripture?

It is clear that the use of the Old Testament[5] by New Testament writ-ers is generally 'pre-critical' in the second sense of the term as I have used it. That is, the lead factor in the use of the Old Testament Scripture passages is the determination of the New Testament writer to make a particular theological or missiological point. The New Testament writers were almost all Jews and saw themselves as inher-itors of the Jewish Scriptures, so the followers of Jesus stand in conti-nuity with those Scriptures. The most obvious example of this is the many times Matthew's Gospel records some action or event in rela-tion to Jesus as taking place 'that the Scriptures might be fulfilled'. The New Testament writers appear to have no hesitation in reading backwards from their experience of Jesus and their encounters in mis-sion, and using the Scriptures to interpret that experience.

One feature of these two kinds of 'pre-critical' reading is common to them both. The direct approach of the first method and the more mediated approach of the second one take seriously the genre of the whole Bible as 'Holy Scripture'. Even before it is opened the Bible is believed by the readers to be the 'word of God'. The expectation is that through encounter with Scripture God will make his will known.

Reading Scripture will lead directly to a renewed call to walk in the ways of God. The connection between encountering holy Scripture and engaging in holy living is assumed. On this reckoning the Bible is *unlike any other kind of literature*.

Having considered two meanings of 'pre-critical' in relation to Bible interpretation we will look briefly at what it means to read the Bible critically. Then we will consider how these different approaches to reading Scripture relate to our question, 'What is a Bible?'

Reading the Bible 'critically' means taking careful account of the historical background, the source documents, the possible authors and their motivations, the way the text has been edited and translated, and how it has been interpreted by other Christians in the past. This involves treating the Bible *as if it is like any other set of ancient texts*. On this reckoning, right interpretation for a critical Christian reader means seeking to discern God's calling as much through the way the text has appeared to change over time, as through the main content of the text itself. It means subjecting it to critical scrutiny using the best tools that scholarship can provide. The history of this process is well written up and evaluated elsewhere.[6] Here we need only to note some key features of this general approach.

First, in order to engage in this kind of biblical study two provisional, but decisive separations have to be made. First, the question 'In what sense is the Bible the word of God?' has to be separated from the questions raised by careful analysis of the text and its background. Second, the interpretation of the Bible has to be separated from the vested interests of the churches and from the spiritual interests of believers. The purpose is to clear away inherited spiritual and ecclesiastical baggage that can get in the way of getting the clearest view of the text itself, by the use of the best methods that a scientific approach can achieve. This is what is meant by a 'modernist' approach. It also means that there can be tensions between the interpretations of critical scholars and those from more 'pre-critical' approaches.

Near the beginning of the modernist approach to the natural sciences in Europe, Nicholas Copernicus (1473–1543) (re-)discovered that the earth orbits around the sun and not the other way round. This posed a major challenge, not only to the established view about astronomy, but also to the way the Bible, with its earth-centred emphasis, was to be interpreted.[7] This serves to illustrate the enormous differences between pre-critical readings on the one hand and historical-critical readings on the other. Pre-critical readings see the Bible as the work of God, revealing his will and his ways to humankind. Critical readings see the Bible as the works of people who are trying to respond to their understanding of 'God' within all the limitations of their times, contexts and capabilities. This means that when they interpret the Bible, readers using a critical approach must use a 'hermeneutic of suspicion' – an interpretive framework that is prepared to question the nature and meaning of the text and to question also the cultural baggage that has given rise to earlier inter-pretations.

The historical-critical approaches offer several advantages. I will highlight five of them.

1. Careful study of the biblical languages and the many manuscripts through which the Bible has come down to us means that we are much better able to be clear about what the text actually says.[8]
2. Technical studies of the forms of the texts and the ways they were edited open up possibilities for richer meanings to be discerned. For example, discoveries that have provisionally associated the major editing of parts of the Pentateuch with the period of the Babylonian Exile have provoked fresh thinking about the theologi-cal and pastoral motivations that may be behind the way texts such as the early chapters of Genesis are expressed.
3. Sociological studies of the contexts of the biblical communities have enabled a clearer understanding of their challenges and opportuni-ties and give clues about their perceptions of God's calling to them. A key example of this is how the sociological and textual studies that were stimulated by the discovery in 1946 of the Dead Sea Scrolls enabled a greater understanding of the Jewish contexts of the Old Testament and New Testament communities, which in turn led to renewed interest in reading the Gospels and Epistles as historically-rooted texts.
4. Literary studies of the genres, linguistic conventions and idioms of the Bible have opened up possible ways of interpretating of texts that would otherwise have remained obscure and inaccessible (and therefore open to projections of fantasy!). For example, locating the later editing of the Book of Daniel in the context of the huge politi-cal and religious crisis of the second century BCE, 'invites us to treat [the] visions typologically and to refer them beyond their context to further oppressors such as Rome and our own oppressors rather than discarding them as failed prophecy.'[9]
5. Studies of the grammar and rhetoric used by biblical writers have opened new ways for understanding the nature of the Gospels.

Richard Burridge has shown, against the previously accepted convention that the Gospels were not written as biographies of Jesus, that in some key respects they *are* closely akin to biographical forms used in relation to leading political figures in the early Christian period.[10]

The separation of Scripture from its essential commitment to being the word of God and to being the closely-guarded property of established churches means that people can stand back from the inherited commitments they bring to the text in order to see more clearly what is there. The purpose, then, of historical-critical studies is to rescue the Bible from its ecclesiastical captivity in order to allow the biblical writers to have their own voices and be heard speaking in their own accents. By getting as close as possible to the original text, genre, and sociological and theological context, critical biblical study aims to place Scripture *prior in time* to the Church and to the doctrines of the Church. When Scripture is allowed its own authentic voices it becomes necessary for the Church to have an adult relationship with an adult Bible instead of the Church speaking on Scripture's behalf like a parent on behalf of an inarticulate child.[11]

Having achieved, for working purposes, the two separations I have described, the next step is to bring close together the things that have been separated. This involves taking stock of what is being learned and seeing how this can speak to the claims of the Bible as God's word and to the ways it can be used in the worship, life and mission of the church. However, this commitment to putting back together what has been separated out for study purposes is not on the agenda of many academic biblical scholars. In any case, academic scholars are as prone to bringing their own prior commitments to their studies as church people are. This has led to calls for the Bible to be rescued from its *academic captivity* so that it can speak in fresh ways to the concerns of ordinary people. A renewed respect for the kinds of 'pre-critical' approaches I outlined earlier is emerging. While historical-critical studies can recognise and illuminate the literary genres of parts of the Bible *as religious literature*, they are not so capable of evaluating the genre of the Bible *as 'Holy Scripture'*. Seeing the Bible as literature is a means of engaging with it using technical and cultural tools of interpretation. Seeing the Bible as Scripture means reading it with the commitments of faith.

Interpreting the Bible with spiritual and theological integrity involves holding together the findings of historical-critical studies and the faith commitments that are part and parcel of what it means to be people of God. For example, Anthony Thiselton, a leading Christian thinker in Britain, has made it his life's work to combine exacting analysis of New Testament text and detailed study of the philosophy of interpretive methods, with a strong commitment to Christian teaching, preaching and leadership.[12] In the mid-1990s Walter Brueggemann took on a task that would have been regarded with deep suspicion by some scholars of the previous decades, of writing a *'Theology* of the Old Testament'.[13] It should be obvious by now that one of the questions pastoral practice must ask concerns how the Bible can be taken seriously *both* as the writings of communities of people in the distant past *and* as holy Scripture.

Scripture as Canon

The most important of the questions that came out of the expanding mission and pastoral practices of the early church was how to maintain the true foundation witness to Jesus Christ. With the church expanding fast, questions were bound to come up about which parts of the Jewish inheritance of Jesus and the first Christians must be held firmly onto and which bits could be left behind. An example of this process at work is seen in the 'Council of Jerusalem' in Acts 15. Here the question of what disciplines should be required of Gentile converts to what was still a deeply Jewish gospel is considered by the leaders of the first generation church. It is impossible to overstate the importance of the decision they took. If the decision had gone the other way Christianity would have remained a Jewish sect and probably fizzled out. As it was, the Christian way was opened to anybody, whether Jewish or not. This decision made the Gentile converts one with the Jewish Christians in their commitment to Jesus Christ, and in a real sense the inheritors of the Hebrew Scriptures as they were at that time. The question of how to reinterpret the Scriptures in the light of the coming of Christ and the gospel mission across boundaries of ethnic and religious cultures became inescapable.

When they took on the task of interpreting Scripture in the light of their new mission, Christian preachers and thinkers came slap up against the problem that some of the contents of the Old Testament seems light years away from the values of Jesus Christ. What for instance are Christians to make of the story of God staying silent while Jephthah carries out the human sacrifice of his only child? (Judges 11:29). This was too much for Marcion, a leader of Gentile Christians in mid-second century Rome. He took the view that the

Old Testament, as the product of some lower level spiritual being, has been superseded by the greatly superior revelation that came through Jesus, so most of it could be abandoned.[14]

The stakes were high and this accounts for the heat and passion that were such a feature of the Councils of the early Church whose deliberations leave us generally unruffled today. The quest to establish what could properly be called 'Holy Scripture' and what could properly be called 'Christian' came directly out of the experiences of mission and the marginality of dispersed communities of Christians during the first three centuries CE. Reaching agreement on the texts of what have become known as the catholic Creeds and agreeing the boundaries of the Canon of Scripture were among the most urgent tasks facing the Councils of the early church. The hard question of how to relate gospel, culture and Scripture was as lively an issue in the early church as it is in Britain and North America today. Maintaining the authenticity of the Church's witness literally depended on resolving this issue.

Alongside the catholic Creeds the Canon of Scripture[15] establishes the base for what counts as the authentic foundation for the worship, preaching, ethics, witness and practice of the Church for all Christians for all time. This seems to lay down the law and demand absolute conformity as the cost of being Christian. That would be as terrible as it is unnecessary. For Christian pastoral practice today I suggest that the notion of the Canon of Scripture needs to develop a connected but much livelier purpose – that of *disruption.* To open up this sense of disruption I want to suggest three roles the Canon of Scripture has to play for twenty-first century Christians.

Connecting Believers of Bible Times with Believers Today

First, the Canon offers a living connection between the faith and witness of Christians today and the women and men whose conversations, actions and struggles we read about in the Old and the New Testament. The story of the *Aqqeda*, the sacrifice of Isaac (Genesis 22:1ff), connects us to people whose thought forms and values are strange, confusing, disturbing. The story of the rejection of Hagar (Genesis 21:9ff) leaves us revolted by the thought that there could be any serious link between the call of God and Abraham's rejection of the woman who gave him his first born son. Scripture connects us to a world of compromise and double-think in which we fear to accept that we are ourselves involved. The account of the disciples in the upper room after Jesus has died (John 20:19ff) connects us to our own closed in-ness and our need for the word of peace from the risen Lord. The words to the angel of the church at Laodicea (Revelation 3:14ff) connects us to the insipidness of the spirituality of many who claim to have a living faith in Christ. The stories, sayings, prayers and visions that make up the Bible are stories that connect me to communities that I belong to. There is a familiarity and a strangeness here that makes for disruption.

This is well captured by Rowan Williams:

> We do not know how to deal properly with Paul in his most ram-pantly masculine moods; we do not know how to deal with some texts on sexuality; we do not know how to cope with the violence of so much of Hebrew Scripture. We say the psalms . . . and quite often find ourselves wishing unspeakable plagues on our ene-mies. All the time we need to remember what kind of humanity it is in which, to which and through which God speaks: a broken humanity, a humanity badly equipped to receive God's liberty.[16]

Connecting Believers Today

Second, the Canon forms a connection between communities of believers in the present. This is an obvious point that I will explore more fully in chapter 6. Across the millions of Christian communities, speaking thousands of different languages, set in different cultural, political and economic circumstances, the Bible is in principle com-mon to all. Christians presuppose that because the message of salva-tion through Jesus Christ is universal in its scope, the Bible is universal in its relevance and application. But this universality of Scripture has to be held together with the rootedness of Scripture in locality. Although there are substantial collections of texts in the Bible without any time or place reference, most of the Bible stories and say-ings are linked with particular people and tied in with particular places and times. Granted that these connections are often difficult to link with corroborative evidence from elsewhere, the intention is clear enough. It is to confirm that the God deals with real people in real places in real time. The different communities of Christians are as dif-ferent from each other as chalk and cheese, so they read the same Bible differently. There is a world of difference between engaging with the Bible in the structured context of a church service in a wealthy neighbourhood and reading the same Bible in a group in a *barrio* where all the people present are out of work and hungry.

Because it connects present-day Christians with each other as well as with Jews and Christians of the past, the Bible opens the way for a belonging that transcends not only differences of culture and language, but also historical time. Here again, there is a familiarity and a strangeness that makes for disruption.

Canon as Gift

Third, the Canon serves to confront Christians with questions of who they are, what they stand for and how they live in relation to other people and to God. This is because the Bible comes to us as something that is *given*. This was brought home to me when a Muslim friend gave me an Arabic Bible for Christmas. He inscribed in it, 'I thought the best present for a man of God are the words of God . . .'. I can neither read nor speak Arabic. I held this precious book with its moving and challenging inscription, but its script is utterly foreign to me. This quality of the Canon of Scripture as something both given and foreign that confronts and threatens to disrupt our thinking, lifestyle and motivations is probably the most important factor in Christians' inheritance of the Bible. The Bible looks us in the face and challenges us to understand what word God wants us to hear and receive today. We are not free to invent our own Bibles to suit ourselves. We are simply faced with the Bible we have got.

This givenness of Scripture is reinforced in churches that use lectionaries and other systematic reading schemes. Whatever the worshipper's state of mind or faith they are simply presented with Scripture as it stands. This is a significant feature of church services and it provokes a range of reactions in both readers and hearers. In response to the generality of Bible readings in church, it is not all that difficult when the reader says, 'This is the Word of the Lord' to respond, 'Thanks be to God'. However when a particularly tough passage is read out – Jesus saying that you can't be fit for the kingdom of heaven if you don't hate your father and mother and sister and brother – it can be hard for the reader not to inflect the words differently – 'This is the Word of the Lord?' and for the hearers to respond with a puzzled, 'Oh well, Thanks be to God.' This givenness of the Canon also has the familiarity and strangeness that makes for disruption.

For some Christians the fact that the Bible exists as a Canon with fixed boundaries leads to the expectation that it can be encountered as a monolithic whole so that it should be possible to discover a harmonisation of spirituality and doctrine across the range of its different parts. The logic works like this: God is consistent in his speaking and acting, and since the Bible was written through the inspiration of the Holy Spirit, we should expect the message of the Bible to be clear and unambiguous. Scripture speaks with one voice, the voice of God and this is heard most clearly through Jesus who is the Word of God. Readers of Scripture who seek to be close to God and open to the inspiration of the Holy Spirit will be able to hear clearly God's will and God's call.

This position is seductively clear. Until, that is, we put another question that pastoral practice asks of the Bible. This concerns the contexts and attitudes of the people who actually wrote it. They brought to their task their roots in their culture, their fallibilities, the axes they wanted to grind, as well as their faith in God. This presents a problem for people who want to propose that the Bible is without error. How can Scripture – the word of God who is infallible – be also the fallible words of people? One solution was proposed in the first and second centuries CE by both Philo and Athenagoras. They suggested that God breathed through the writers of Scripture as a flute player breathes through his flute. But this idea causes more problems than it solves. Moule quotes John Zeisler:

> It is not that God controls or supersedes my decisions and so on, so that I think they are mine though they are really being manipulated by God, but that my genuine freedom, my character, my personality, and all my decisions are mine only because God enables them to be so . . . God . . . does not threaten man's humanness or freedom or integrity – he guarantees them!

Moule continues, 'Thus a conception of inspiration as the mechanical prevention of error is not only an illegitimate stretching of the meaning of the word; it is a sub-personal, sub-theistic conception of God: least of all is it compatible with a fully Christian understanding of the Word made flesh.'[17]

And then there is the Bible's unawareness of its own completed existence. A simple illustration may help make clear what I mean. As an evangelical pastor I had grown used to thinking of the Bible as something that is whole, complete, coherent when a rather naïve and totally obvious thought occurred to me with real force. Nobody whose name appears in the Bible ever read it whole. Most of them never even read the stories that describe their experience, so they didn't know the end of the story while it was still in process. What the

Bible offers is reflections, testimonies, prayers, poems and chronicles of people's experiences of the presence, the silence, the speaking, the grace, holiness, sternness, gentleness and deliverance of God. It is also directly the record of their perceptions of their personal and community histories, present circumstances and future hopes. The Bible gives a sense of communities and persons being open to the discovery of who God is and what God is doing. This means that attempts at harmonisation between parts of the Bible that are saying different things are not only doomed to failure, but are actually a denial of the character of Scripture as open, searching, welcoming and challenging.

Certainly there is already awareness in the Bible of the idea and importance of Scripture. We see this in the beginning of the reforms led by Josiah (2 Chronicles 34:14ff); the reading of the prophets (Luke 4:16ff), the struggles of the disciples to discern the relationship between the human Jesus and the source of his teaching (Matthew 13:53); the repeated assertion that in the actions of Jesus the Scriptures were being fulfilled; the hint by Paul of the importance of his parchments (2 Timothy 4:13). But the lasting impression is of writings that were regarded as fresh, relevant, open to discussion and discernment, and – certainly in the New Testament – still incomplete. In other words the voices of what was accepted as Scripture and the voices of the present were involved in a series of conversations designed to discern, celebrate *and question* claims about the actions of people in response to the call of God. This essential liveliness of Scripture means that the disruptive givenness of the Bible must be received as the call to explore the mystery of life with God rather than merely as ground-rules for well-behaved believers.

Canon and Conversation

Having a Canon of Scripture is deeply paradoxical. One the one hand the Canon of Scripture is fixed and unalterable.[18] The fixing of the Canon was the work of the Church. To this extent the Church comes *before* the Bible and is the controller of the boundaries of Scripture. On the other hand, Scripture comes *before* the Church in the sense that it arose directly out of the inheritance the faith and the mission of the first Christians. Scripture both illuminates and challenges the claims Christians make about themselves, so the relationship between the Bible and the Church must be more like an inspiring and argumentative tussle than a pious status quo. The journey towards fixing the Canon involved testimonies, debates, passionate disputes. What is on offer for twenty-first century Christians from Scripture is the call to conversations with the people whose experiences, concerns, questions, hopes and confusions gave rise to the writings in the first place. Scripture as Canon, then, is *both* a means of defending what counts as authentic apostolic witness, and a provocation to conversations that can lead somewhere.

The Canon of Scripture is likely to be challenging as a conversation partner. For the same Canon that contains the parable of the prodigal son (Luke 15); the hymn of the humility of Christ (Philippians 2: 5ff) and Psalm 23 also contains 'Samuel hewed Agag in pieces before the Lord in Gilgal' (1 Samuel 15:33) and the murder of Sisera with a tent peg by Jael in Judges 4:21. It is not surprising therefore, that Christians have tended to develop their own 'canon within a canon'. For example, evangelicals tend to prefer the Pauline Epistles to other parts of the New Testament because of the emphasis on justification by grace through faith in Romans and Galatians. Some liberals prefer the Sermon on the Mount in Matthew 5—7. Some liberation theologians prefer Exodus and texts related to the Babylonian exile. So it is important, when considering our question 'What is a Bible?', to recognise that one of the results of Scripture coming to us as a fixed Canon is that it comes to us *whole*. This is enormously significant. Just as one of the clichés of religious debate concerns the tendency of people to make God in their own image, there is a similar tendency among Christians to remake Scripture in their own images. Further, the fact that Scripture speaks with many voices means that engaging with Scripture is much more like engaging in conversation than making use of a 'thing' like some kind of tool.

As well as the Canon two other things are 'given'. These are today's hearers and readers with their experiences, opinions, values and preferences; and Bible readers in the past who have left us the legacies of their ways of reading Scripture. So when the Bible is being read there are not just one or two voices to be heard, but many. In one place where I worked there was a strike of coal miners that caused deep bitterness in our community. A bishop came to help us work with the people on both sides. After days of very difficult meetings he said, 'We've spent the whole week listening – we've been sweating with listening.' Really listening to Scripture is as committed and as serious as that. This careful listening is a lot more than developing an open-minded piety within Christian communities. Real commitment to treating the Bible as God's genuinely open book has profound effects on how we relate to neighbours who share our faith, but in another part of the Christian tradition; have no faith at all; or are followers of another world faith.

Why Is a Bible Necessary?

It is possible to have something approaching religious faith without reference to any holy Scriptures, but the followers of the three Semitic world faiths are 'people of the book'. Christians share with Jews roots in the Hebrew Scriptures. Muslims find one of the five pillars of their faith in the Holy Qur'an. To put it simply, holy Scripture and holy living belong together in the same 'conversation'. In other words, accepting the Bible as foundational for faith and witness is basic to the identity of Christians *as Christians*. Talk about 'foundations' suggests something solid and immovable, but as we have seen this particular foundation is much more open, dynamic, lively, multi-vocal as it speaks of the one God and the things of God.

There are a number of markers for the assessing the genuineness of Christian faith as *Christian* faith. These include: baptism in the name of the holy Trinity; accepting the Bible as foundational for the life of faith lived in community with the people of God; sharing belief in the 'catholic' Creeds as the agreed summaries of faith; and participation in the worship, life and witness of the Church. If you take any one of these four 'table legs' away, the table may stay a table but it will be harder to share dinner at it. The fact that Christians universally agree that the Bible should be translated into local vernaculars,[19] gives the clue to the openness to interpretation that is the hall-mark of how they are to relate to Scripture.

Not in Front of the Children?

I referred earlier to the tendency of pastors to keep what they have learned from historical-critical studies of the Bible away from their congregations. When challenged about this, they tend to speak about protecting their congregations from unnecessary detail that would be too difficult for them to grasp. It is not the role of the pastor to foist irrelevant academic detail on to hard-pressed congregations, but we do need to ask what it is that congregations are being protected from by this rather patronising approach. Suppressing or concealing realities about Scripture from the congregation, so that readings are compelled to remain in conformity with established conventions of piety, seems to risk making the Bible increasingly inaccessible and irrelevant to the realities of practical living. Who is defending whom from what? 'Faithfully guarding the word of truth' is a far cry from concealing the truth about the word in the first place. This approach risks limiting the fuller engagement with the Bible that could come from honest exploration of questions that are raised by the forms and changes as well as by the contents of the text.

Christians engage in source and form criticism every time they take their mail to the kitchen table. They can tell even before they open them which of the packages is likely to contain an electricity bill, a holiday brochure, a letter from Aunt Margaret, the answer to a legal query or news that they have just won a cash prize. They engage in redaction criticism every time they watch two TV news channels or read two newspapers reporting the same event. They engage with different genres of communication every time they channel-hop using the remote control. Moreover, when Christians listen to the reading of Scripture or preaching and teaching, especially in settings where they keep silent while the pastor speaks, they engage in processes of often subconscious discrimination about which bits of what they hear scratch where they itch and which parts they can safely leave alone.

The issue of how best to address congregations' questions about the content, development and interpretation of Scripture is really about honesty and the politics of disclosure. It is not a uniquely twenty-first century issue as the history of the suppression of the Bible in English during the early Reformation period indicates. At bottom it is a question about who the Bible belongs to and who has the authority to interpret it. In other words it is a question about the politics of knowledge and church order. The question of who 'owns' the Bible will be the subject of chapter 3, but first we must ask how the Bible relates to the Word of God.

CHAPTER 2

How Does the Bible Relate to the Word of God?

Hearers of the Word

The claim that the Bible is the 'word of God' raises a whole lot of questions. Is it God's first word, God's only word, God's last word? What kind of word is it anyway? Throughout Christian history the vast majority of believers have experienced the Bible as *spoken* rather than as written word. This holds true even when literacy is almost universal and the level of personal Bible ownership is the highest it has ever been. Christians are, and always have been, much more likely to hear and sing the words of Scripture in public worship and see its stories in visual art, drama, and (more recently) film than they are to read the Bible for themselves or in small groups at home. Certainly the spoken or sung word, the visual art, drama and film, will all have some kind of closer or more distant relationship to the written word of the Bible itself. But when we are trying to understand the kinds of questions pastoral practice puts to the Bible it is essential to notice that when the two meet, they normally meet in the lively interactions of speech, song, stories and dramas that are taking place in the present.

The main emphasis in the Bible itself is on the *spoken* word. The focus is on what happens when the word God speaks is allowed its freedom and its fruitfulness, is welcomed or resisted, is clearly heard or barely audible amongst all the other words that are competing for attention. Even the way the Canon is arranged means that the priority belongs to what happens when God speaks. The creation stories in Genesis 1 and 2 with their rhythm of 'and God said . . . and it was so', begin with a kind of manifesto. The chaotic, formless, empty darkness is confronted by the word of God and is compelled to give way to order, shape, richness and light. The stories of the creation and fall are dominated by the spoken word. They come to their climax following the question of whether or not the speaking of God can be trusted as truth: '[the serpent] said to the woman, "Did God say . . . you will not die, for God knows that when you eat of it your eyes will be opened and you will be like God . . ."' (Genesis 3:1–5).

The patriarchal narratives, the giving of the Law, the making and renewing of the covenant, the calling and the preaching of the prophets, the love poems, proverbs and psalms are all presented as reports of the spoken word of God and the spoken responses of people finding their voices in the same conversations. The fact that the books of Joshua, Judges, Samuel and Kings, normally thought of by Christians as 'historical', are classified in the Hebrew Bible as the 'former prophets' serves to emphasise the point.

We find the same emphasis on the spoken word in the New Testament. The Gospels are filled with accounts of Jesus talking with people. Even the descriptive sections are structured around the speaking of Jesus. The Epistles are best thought of as dialogue and preaching materials presented as words 'spoken from a distance'. The two clearest examples of the emphasis on the spoken word in the New Testament are both from Johannine writing. The prologue to the Gospel of John is closely structured in parallel with the opening of Genesis, with its 'In the beginning was the Word' (brilliantly paraphrased in the Scouse Gospel as 'Affore God did owt 'e 'ad summat te say.') The First Letter of John opens 'We declare to you what was from the beginning, what we have heard, what we have seen with our eyes, what we have looked at and touched with our hands, concerning the word of life . . .'

I emphasise this importance of the Bible as *spoken* word because there has been such an emphasis in Christian writing on the Bible as *written word* – as text. The Bible comes as written word because it was first spoken word. Even the less obviously spoken sections of the Old Testament, such as the law codes, are presented in the framework of the speaking of God. In the NRSV 20 out of the 27 chapters of Leviticus begin with a phrase such as, 'The Lord said to Moses . . .', and the ones that don't are continuations of the others. It makes an enormous difference to the way Christians understand the nature of the *Torah* and how Jesus and Paul relate to it in the New Testament, if it is understood primarily in terms of the spoken call of God to live in faithfulness to the covenant; and secondarily as a written code designed to preserve this speaking. Jesus' confrontations with the Pharisees often arose from their apparent failure to recognise that they had allowed the liveliness of the spoken word of God to give way to a rigidity of attitude in responding to the written word.[1]

From the beginning, the word of God is revealed through Scripture as *public utterance*, spoken in the expectation that there will be a response of faithful action by the hearers. As *written word* the Bible is intended to preserve the 'first speaking' of the word of God so that all subsequent speaking of the word can be tested against this foundation. Clearly there will be tension between Scripture experienced as the word of God spoken and sung and as the word of God written, read and studied. Speech is immediate, dynamic, interactive. It is also fragmentary, risky, potentially irresponsible, provisional, difficult to control. Once something is said, it can't be unsaid, but it may also be hard to recall accurately. Speakers can be clear about what they want to say, but that is no guarantee of what the hearers will hear. At least the act of writing does established the text as the agreed basis from which the interpretations of the writers and the readers can begin their conversation. In other words, when we are dealing with Scripture we need to understand that there must be a dynamic relationship between speech and text – between what is received from the past and what is contributed by the present.

The problem arises that in dealing with Scripture, the primacy between speech and text must always belong to the text because that is the foundation of the true speaking. This can lead to a tendency for particular ways of using the written text to squeeze out the liveliness of the speaking that gave rise to it in the first place. The richness of public utterance with its capacity for texture, tone of voice, irony, humour, pathos, argument can give way to a flatness of reading and interpreting the text, especially perhaps when the purpose of the interpretation is to defend some aspect of orthodoxy or right doctrine.

Jesus challenged this tendency towards the flattening of Scripture by injecting a whole new emphasis into the conversation. The conventional rehearsal of what was written is forced to gave way to a much more challenging understanding of the text as he comes 'not to abolish the law and the prophets, but to fulfil [them]' (Matthew 5:17). The examples he chooses are as startling as they are ordinary. They relate to family life, anger and murder; adultery, divorce and re-marriage; swearing oaths and speaking the truth; non-violent resistance to oppression; relationships with neighbours and enemies; almsgiving, prayer and fasting, and how people get the food and clothing they need. All of it leads to the two punch-lines that show where the written inheritance of the *Torah* is intended to lead as results of the practical actions of the people of God: '. . . seek first the kingdom of God and his righteousness, and all these things will be given to you as well' and 'Everyone who hears these words of mind *and does them* . . .' (Matthew 5:21; 7:24). Jesus draws the written and remembered text back into direct speech so that the word of God can challenge people who have been called to faithful living of the *Torah*, but who have settled for low-level and legalistic religious pragmatism. For Jesus, the received text is the foundation for the speaking that makes the word of God able to be heard afresh.

This contrast between the Bible as written word and as spoken word may give a clue to the real differences between the ways in which clergy and church officials on the one hand and lay Christians on the other encounter the Bible. It is important to be cautious here because this can be overstated. But I may not be far wrong in suggesting that from the time when they enter seminary the most intensive experience most clergy have of the Bible is as written text separated from its role as public utterance. Scripture is studied in a private and individual way under the supervision of teachers whose main experience of the Bible may also be as written text separated from its role as public utterance. At the same time, the main experience of the Bible for most church members will be as public utterance that may be more or less closely related to its written foundations. Certainly, seminary students and clergy will also be committed to public worship and the life of prayer; but I think the dynamic may be set whereby clergy tend to experience the text mainly as written word in their study and preparation for preaching, whereas the rest of the church experience it mainly as spoken word. There is potential here for real discovery as congregations explore the creative tensions that arise between these two modes of encountering the Bible as the word of God.

However this kind of shared access to the speaking of the Bible is not always the pattern in churches in Britain. The monopoly of right interpretation is associated with clergy and preachers to such an extent that the speaking of the 'experts' about Scripture is given more weight than the speaking of anybody else about it. There are good reasons for this. Although there is a history of highly effective uneducated itinerant 'charismatic' Bible preachers such as Billy Bray[2] in nineteenth-century Cornwall, congregations have a right to expect their leaders to have done their homework, and to have engaged deeply with the text of the Bible in a way that they themselves may be unable to because of other demands. Being free to engage in this kind of study is one of the reasons church leaders are 'set apart'. From their careful study of the Bible they are called to bring what they have been hearing from the written text to a new stage in the 'conversation' between Scripture and the congregation. But this will mean that the clergy and other church leaders involved in leading Scripture interpretation have to join their own churches so they can hear clearly both Scripture and the real voices of the congregation. A story will give an example of what I mean.

When I was a parish priest I wondered why, although I enjoyed preaching, the sermons seemed not to be connecting very well with the congregation. I simply wasn't making contact most of the time. I remembered that as seminary students we were recommended to go to work with a parishioner about once a month for a whole day so that we could learn to preach better. I found myself spending time with congregation members down a coal mine, up a gantry cleaning street lights, in a classroom studying maths, helping load potatoes in a grocer's store, in a factory that made women's clothes, and in an advertising agency, among other places. The experience transformed the view from the pulpit and made me re-think my approach to working with the people in relation to the Bible. There were so many voices making claims to be heard by these church members about all sorts of important things. Among them were the 'voices' of Scripture. My role was to be involved in the conversations that Scripture is involved in, so that I could help open the way for the voices of Scripture, 'the word of the Lord', to be heard and welcomed. In short, the role is to allow the written word faithfully to have its say in speaking the word of God in a specific locality.

This does not presume a solidity in the written text – the meanings of written text can be almost as labile as live speech. But it is to emphasise the point that the primacy between speech and text must belong to the text because for Christians that is the foundation of 'true speaking' in prayer, worship and testimony. The primacy of the written text means that people are not free to make up their own version of the story of faith, without reference to the Bible, and to claim fairly that the result can be called 'Christian'. Claims for versions of the human story to be considered as genuinely Christian have no option but to allow themselves to be heard and evaluated by reference to the Bible. To put it bluntly, accepting the Bible as 'holy Scripture' is basic to Christian identity. This does not, however, mean a retreat into fundamentalism. But it does mean that we have to consider how the Word of God is revealed through the Bible. I will highlight three traditional ways of associating the word of God with the Bible, then discuss a more recent one.

1. The Bible *Is* the Word of God

The first position makes the Bible and the Word of God virtually identical. The argument is that the contents and the Canon of the Bible came into their present shape through people who were especially inspired by God for this purpose. 2 Timothy 3:16 – 'all Scripture is inspired by God' is taken to apply literally both to the Old Testament and to the documents of the New Testament, even though these were still in the process of formation when this text was written. A sophisticated piece of theological argument is used to back this up. Words in John's Gospel where Jesus says that he speaks the words that are given to him by the Father (John 8:26; 12:49; 17:8) are linked up with the promise of Jesus that 'When the Spirit of truth comes, he will guide you into all the truth . . . he will take what is mine and declare it to you . . .' (John 16:13–15). This is interpreted as the promise that just as the words of Jesus are divine words, through the leading of the Holy Spirit the words of Jesus' disciples that find their way into Scripture will also be the words of God. Writing from a theological position consistent with *The Chicago Statement on Biblical Inerrancy* (1976), Timothy Ward expresses this with almost alarming frankness:

> [Jesus] is explaining that, after his ascension, certain human beings will be given by the Holy Spirit words to speak that are of equal divine origin and character to words uttered directly by the Father or by the Son. The fact that all the disciples remain sinners till the day they die does not alter the fact that, if they faithfully pass on what the Spirit gives them to say, their words are God's own words, just as much as the Ten Commandments or the Beatitudes . . . However, the full implications of this promise do not apply to every believer.[3]

Ward argues that since the same Holy Spirit who inspired the speaking of Jesus and the disciples also inspired the speaking of people in the Old Testament, the Hebrew Scriptures also have a special status in relation to the speaking of God. '. . . for Jesus, the Old Testament is not just historically true. It is also . . . of divine origin, in the strong sense of that claim: *whatever it says is what God says.*'[4] This argument is dynamically very close to orthodox teaching about the origin and authority of the Holy Qur'an. To be fair, in his article Ward is trying to pack a great deal into a small space; and the later part of his piece locates his argument within a careful exposition of what it means to understand the Bible in the light of 'speech-act' theory. This is the notion that the basic unit of language-in-use is not the individual word but the 'speech-act'. 'Speech-acts are a kind of extension of the self . . .' so the speaking of God through the writers of Scripture takes place under the inspiration of the Holy Spirit as a kind of extension of the character of God, whose words are being spoken by this means. This places a great responsibility on the interpreters of Scripture, for engaging with its words opens up a direct encounter with the character of God. Ward is keen to rely on a very strong notion of the providence of God working through the lives of the Bible writers, translators and interpreters. This leads him to insist on the notions of the inerrancy and infallibility of the Bible that were fully worked out as late as the nineteenth century by writers such as Hodge and Warfield in the context of the science v. Scripture debate.

This approach to describing how the word of God comes through Scripture has the merit of being straightforward, direct, understandable. It puts the obligation on the hearer to take the words of Scripture seriously as the words that bring the call of God. But it raises particular problems when it comes to interpreting passages where God is presented as requiring attitudes and practices that most people today would regard as racist, sexist, discriminatory or violent. It will be clear that when people come to the Bible seeking to know the will of God, they are faced not just with a technical task, but with a theological and ethical one. Hard questions have to be asked, such as, 'if the words of the Bible are the words of God, what kind of God do people hear speaking in Scripture?'; and 'if different groups of people hear the word of God differently from each other, who is to decide which hearing is the right one and what criteria will they need to use?'

2. The Bible *Reveals* the Word of God

This position also associates the Bible with the coming of the word of God, but does not seek to identify them with each other. The argument is that the Bible, *taken as a whole*, is inspired by the Holy Spirit and so reveals the word of God. There is no claim here that the words of God and the words of Scripture are necessarily the same. It is acknowledged that even if the Bible as whole is inspired, some parts of it will prove to be more inspiring than others. The whole Bible has to be held together because the situation may arise where texts that have remained dormant become suddenly filled with power and make their presence felt. This is what happened in the 1970s–90s with liberationist readings of Exodus and Revelation in South America and

South Africa; and, with a broader engagement with the biblical text, in feminist re-readings of Old Testament passages, such as the stories of Hagar, Ruth and Esther.

The idea that the Bible reveals the word of God, and therefore the will of God, provides the foundation for discovering what Christians believe, and for their commitments to true prayer and right action. In traditional terms the Bible is the foundation of doctrine, mission and pastoral care and spirituality. All of this can be explored intellectually by looking at the way the Bible has been used at different times in history. But there is a mystical or spiritual element too. For ordinary believers, the dominant mode of engaging with Scripture is in the context of their shared worship and lived spirituality. The common experience of Christians is that the Canon of Scripture provides the basis for seeking God's word of guidance, challenge, comfort and hope among the messiness of daily life. There may be other places where you could look for these things, so the argument goes, but you cannot guarantee finding them except in the Scriptures that focus on the coming of Jesus Christ. A pious way of expressing this is to say that the word of God as revealed in Scripture in the past becomes a word for living now. Although there is a certain circularity to this argument – the givenness of the Bible leads Christians to find what they expect to find in it – the claim that the Bible reveals the word of God is based in the traditions of Christian orthodoxy and the present experiences of believers.

How the actual contents of the biblical books are regarded is important for this view. The Bible has no place for religion conceived as a special kind of experience separated from the rest of life. The central teaching of Old Testament prophets such as Hosea and Amos, and of Jesus himself, is firmly that God's holiness and the ordinary lives of people belong together. The catalogue of biblical references to tents, houses, boundary markers, food, clothing, warfare, employment, slavery, etc., signals that the word of God comes as the call to live in faithfulness to his speaking among the ordinariness of daily life. Furthermore, the passages that speak of warfare, violence, revenge, bitterness and despair are also important because they speak directly about human experience. Indeed, some of them witness to the religious claims that perpetrating violent acts on others is done in response to God's call. This is very familiar in the twenty-first century where terrorist and governmental acts of violence may be accompanied by claims to be acting in the name of 'God'. Christians cannot get away from the hard moral political and ethical questions of how a Bible that contains this kind of material can be said to reveal the word of God.

A common way of dealing with these questions is to resort to the idea of 'progressive revelation'. This is the notion that the parts of the Old Testament where people act with extreme violence, apparently in obedience to the will of God, witness to 'primitive' understandings of the character of God. These have been superseded by the more 'civilised' insights that we find in the later parts of Scripture, especially in the New Testament. In a word, the later revelation is more true to the character of God than the earlier revelation. There may be truth in this, but it throws up more questions rather than solving all the problems. For example, how does the idea of progressive revelation square up with the idea of the consistency of the character of God? Might it be better to put the onus of proof on people who claim they are acting according to the will of God, and talk about *progression of perceptions* over time?

This hard question leads us to face up to another, that the idea of progressive perception itself rests on an optimistic assumption about human nature and whether people really are made more holy by their claimed experiences of the speaking of God. It is convenient to claim that, in carrying out some aggressive act, a person or a community is doing the will of God. The responsibility is transferred onto the divine will. The buck really does stop with God. Where this strategy is put together with claims that the word of God has been received and his will discerned with absolute clarity the theological foundations for religious terrorism are beginning to be laid. The reality of religiously-motivated violence carried out by Christians as well as people of other faiths at the start of the twenty-first century should at least make us suspicious of the kind of optimism that lies behind the notions of progressive revelation or perception. By asking these kinds of questions as they engage with Scripture, Christians may be able to move beyond the biblical rhetoric and see some of the shady dynamics that are really at work. When people welcome the Bible into their talking about some of the harsh realities of human behaviour, they become open to faith conversations that can go way beyond recycling old opinions and familiar arguments. There can be fresh listening and talking where the word of God can speak with compelling clarity and relevance.

It will be clear that people holding to this second way of understanding the relationship between the text of Scripture and the word of God will be less likely to be concerned with minutiae of how some of the actual words of Scripture are to be interpreted. They are likely to see the very presence of Scripture in the conversation as almost as significant as what it might have to say. As I have tried to show, this does not mean that what the text says can be disregarded. But it does mean that when people make an authority or truth claim based on a particular passage, they will take care to hear what else Scripture has to say about it. They will also want to know whether other parts of Scripture *that do not directly mention the topic under discussion* may also have something important to say. For example, Stephen Fowl explores claims that the section in Acts 10—15 about the relation between Jewish and Gentile believers may be held together in the debate about homosexuality alongside texts that refer directly to it.[5]

The capacity to reveal the word of God is not a quality that Scripture has apart from the people who open it. It takes at least two to have a conversation. An essential requirement is that the speakers offer one another the generous hospitality of attentive listening. This generous hospitality that makes conversation creative is what the Bible brings when it is allowed to speak as open text rather than closed text. Fowl sees this hospitality as an essential quality of the 'friendship' which makes a genuine participation in conversation with Scripture possible:

> . . . as related in Acts, the very manner in which the Gentiles were included as full members of the people of God presupposes a whole set of ecclesiological practices which are largely absent from Christianity in the US. Most churches do not train and nurture people in forming the sorts of friendships out of which testimony about the Spirit's work might arise.[6]

3. The Bible *Contains* the Word of God

A can could be said to contain tomato soup and nothing else. A box could be said to contain pencils, but that doesn't mean that it might not also contain some crayons and a discarded piece of chewing gum. In relation to Scripture the first of these is the same as holding the view that the Bible *is* the word of God, so I will concentrate here on the second meaning of 'contain'.

The idea that the Bible contains the word of God alongside a lot of other stuff that it contains reflects a major tradition of the church and the way most people use the Bible in practice. The *Thirty-Nine Articles of Religion* which is a foundation document of the Anglican Church steers clear of the idea that the Bible is in itself the word of God.

Instead it declares that 'Holy Scripture *containeth* all things necessary to salvation . . .' (Article VI) and goes on to accept that although the parts of the Old Testament law relating to ceremonies and rites 'do not bind Christian men' the moral law does (Article VII). This is more than just one of the nooks and crannies of church history, because these Articles were formulated by Protestant Reformers in the seventeenth century when they were at the height of their influence. At a time when you would expect to find them at their most confident and conservative, you find them accepting that some parts of the Bible itself are more important than others for Christian belief and practice. This begs the question of how you tell which is which. The people who compiled the Articles wanted to differentiate between the ceremonial and ritual aspects of the Pentateuch and the moral commandments. Their approach raises the question of whether this difference is theologically valid and if it could be applied to other things that the Bible speaks about.

In the day-to-day practice of Christians this is exactly what happens. Particular passages of Scripture are more frequently read than others in public worship or personal devotions. You can buy Bibles that have 'the most important parts', such as key prophecies from the Old Testament or the words of Jesus, printed in red. Many Christians will underline sections in their Bibles that they find especially helpful. This process of selection may be largely unconscious and informal. But it is also formalised in official church lectionaries where priority is given to some parts of the Bible, especially the New Testament, while others parts are absent. These are different versions of the idea of a 'canon within the Canon'. You can tell which parts of the Bible are a particular church's 'canon within the Canon' by noting which parts of Scripture they use most often and why.

But there are two other meaning of *contains* that we need to think about. Cell 25 contains prisoner Bloggs. All of prisoner Bloggs is in Cell 25. When we apply this to how the Bible reveals the word of God we have to ask this hard question: if not all of the Bible is to be counted as the word of God for today because some of it has become less relevant through the coming of Jesus Christ and changes of time and culture, can we say nevertheless that *all* of God's word is to be found in the Bible? The answer of most parts of church tradition to this question is an unqualified 'yes'.[7] Although God and therefore God's word is independent of the Bible, God has chosen to reveal his full character, will, and calling to humankind through the Scriptures.

There are three reasons to be cautious about this:

1. *The church has always held that God's 'speaking' can be recognised, quite apart from Scripture, through encounter with the natural world.*

   Because the natural world and everything in it is the creation of God; and because people are made in the image of God, it is possible to discern the character, the holiness, the purposes and the call of God through seeing these things for what they really are – manifestations of the love and creativity of God. This is the departure point for Paul's argument in Romans (1—3) that all have sinned and fallen short of the glory of God.

2. *The church has always held that God has continued guiding it and speaking to it even after the end of the New Testament period in fulfilment of the promise of Jesus that the 'Holy Spirit will guide you into all truth'.*

   For the Roman Catholic and Orthodox churches the developing traditions of the church are held to contain further revelation of the working of God. Disputes about the methods, reality and status of such further revelation are still at the heart of many arguments about what counts as right Christian belief and practice today. However, even in Protestant churches this possibility has been maintained, especially in relation to the developing patterns and forms of their mission and ministry activities.

3. *The first generations of Christians lived in a world which was just as religiously pluralistic, though in different ways, as twenty-first century Europe and North America.*

   Paul himself in Athens (Acts 17:22ff) and a century later, Justin Martyr,[8] recognised that God could speak through other religions, though they held that this was in a muffled and indistinct form. The compilers of the *Articles* were well aware of this when they chose to use the word *'contains'*. Their assumption was that God's character guarantees that God's true speaking through nature, the properly-based traditions of the church, and other faiths will always be consonant with God's speaking in the Bible.

Ever since the writing of John's Gospel it has been a central part of Christian teaching to refer to Jesus of Nazareth as the 'Word of God'. But you don't have to read very far into the Gospels to see that this 'Word of God' has some strange ways of speaking and chooses some strange people to be his hearers. The whole theological sequence from incarnation, through companionship, teaching and testimony, suffering, death and even resurrection is underlined by the themes of ambiguity and self-limitation. The classic recognition of this is Paul's hymn to the humility of Christ in Philippians 2:5–11. The notion that the

Bible *contains* the word of God in the sense that God's definitive self-revelation is limited to what can be found in Scripture is of enormous theological importance. It is the foundational idea behind the development and fixing of the Canon of Scripture and the energy source for claims about the authority of Scripture. The authority of the Bible derives from God whose word it contains, and from the solidarity of present day Christians with the early communities of believers who collected, edited and wrote it, not from some quasi-magical quality of the text itself.

The final meaning of *contains* can be shown by saying that a country contains the communities of people who live within its borders. There are many differences between people living in different parts of the land – racial, first language, economic, employment, inherited traditions, environment, etc. The well-being of the country depends on how different groups can relate to each other, serve one another's needs, depend on one another for their prosperity and protection and enrich one another by their cultural life. The health and welfare of the citizens depends not only on laws to limit the extent of injustice but, more importantly, on the essential hospitality and trust that enables different people to offer one another space to grow and prosper. 'Contained' within a country are people who depend for their essential prosperity on a shared sense of freedom, openness, opportunity, interaction.

This meaning of '*contains* the word of God', applied to the Bible, serves as an invitation to enter the 'country', and experience the generosity and hospitality (and the defensiveness and wariness that foreigners sometimes attract) that it offers. Here are opportunities to hear the speaking of God and of other people of God that sound familiar, but are also profoundly strange. Here are invitations to stay and accept these people as one's own people, this God as 'our' God. Here are invitations to establish foundations for your faith, but also the roots of who you are and what you are for. Just as there will always be times of tension between immigrants and their adopted country, however hospitable it proves to be, there must also be creative tension between contemporary believers and the foreign-but-familiar world of the Bible and the God whose word it 'contains'. This meaning of *contains* expects that engagement with Scripture will be freely chosen, attitudinally open, interactive – but this does not carry with it any sense that the Bible is less foundational for faith than other understandings of 'contains'. The 'country' of the Bible is still 'there' when today's foreigner-citizens arrive to explore it, and they need the humility, hospitality and generosity of spirit to open themselves to its strange ways of speaking.

I should be clear that asking exactly how hearing the Bible relates to hearing the word of God can only take us so far if it remains just a question about technical process. You can study the Bible phenomenologically – as a kind of 'thing' – great literature, ancient writings, a religious artefact, etc. But when you ask how the Bible relates to the word of God you are asking *theological* questions and they are about faith seeking understanding. In this chapter I have used metaphors of canned soup, a pencil case, a prison cell and a foreign country to explore different aspects of the question. There are many other possibilities. Whether you see the words of Scripture as themselves the words of God, or favour one of the 'container' images, you are claiming that the Bible as written text and as the word of God belong together and they are to be received together. And that is a *faith claim*.

This faith claim takes the ordinary human evidence, the fact and content of the Bible, then does two things with it. First, it assumes that the Bible exists because God has something to say that people have heard and responded to in the past. Second, it assumes both that that particular speaking of God had definitive significance for the people who first received it *and* that through Scripture God may have something definitive *and similar* to say to people today. Whichever metaphor people use to understand how the words of the Bible relate to the word of God, it must hold these two aspects of this faith claim together. Metaphors are important because they are suggestive and open-ended, rather than definitive and final. Many of the theological problems between people who hold different views of the relation between the Bible and the word of God centre around the hard question of where symbolic speech such as metaphor ends, and definitive speech begins.

Scripture as Sacrament

Stephen Wright distinguishes between 'using' and 'receiving' Scripture. '"Receiving"' any literary text . . . entails a readiness to be immersed both in "the words on the page" and the realities to which they point. It implies that the reader (or hearer) is drawn out of themselves in a transcendental moment of encounter.'[9] Wright uses the theological model of *sacrament* to explore the relationship between the words of Scripture and the speaking of God. A sacrament is a kind of open container within which the drama of holy words and of divine and human actions are held together.[10] It is also an 'effective action' in the technical sense that it is intended to deliver what it symbolises.

Sacraments are 'holy mysteries' in the theological sense of moments of decisive personal encounter with God. Everyday things like bread and wine, water and oil, human hands, become signs of the transformations God brings about through new birth, blessing, forgiveness, suffering and healing. But they are not pieces of magic. They do not 'work' apart from the speaking of God and the response of faith. Sacraments cannot be fully explained rationally any more than a work of art or a joke can. A joke stops being funny if you explain it. The essential 'holy mystery' of the sacrament is lost. The model of 'sacrament' as a container holding together a number of different sorts of reality has possibilities for helping us understand the relation between hearing the words of Scripture and receiving the word of God. Wright brings this out as he explores the affirmation, 'This is the word of the Lord' at the end of Bible readings in church services:

> Understood . . . as sacramental language, 'This is the word of the Lord' is precisely the *saviour* of Scripture from the irrelevance and offensiveness into which it would inevitably sink without it. It is only because we say *sacramentally* that the Bible is the word of the Lord that we can *both* continue to use it as formative and central in Christian life and worship, *and* treat it seriously as a collection of human documents . . . Treated . . . as a sacramental affirmation which heightens the possible *contrast* between what Scripture says and what God says, 'This is the word of the Lord' affirms the gracious truth that God continues to speak through an amazing variety of fallible human viewpoints.[11]

Wright has put his finger on a very important principle here. It is this. When you bring together the faith commitment that the Bible is or reveals or contains the word of God with the question about how this can happen, you need a particular way of talking about it. This has to be able to hold together possibilities of comparisons and parallels between Scripture and the experience of the hearer with possibilities of contrast, confusion and mystery. In the Bible Christians find many passages that offer comparisons and parallels between the experiences of the writers and their own experiences.

For example, somebody seeking assurance that they are fully accepted and understood by God might find comfort through the testimony–prayer of Psalm 139, or through God's speaking to Elijah in the 'still small voice' in 1 Kings 19:12. But the same person is likely to find challenging the contrast between their present experience and the sense of bitter and violent protest at the end of Psalm 137; or by Elijah's wholesale slaughter of the priests of Baal (just five paragraphs earlier in the NRSV) before God meets him on the mountain. If claims that connect the contents of the Bible with the speaking of God to people today are to have any credibility, they will have to be made in language that can cope with parallels, contrasts and mystery. Language that depends on precise definitions and makes claims for the full knowability of the meaning of the text always needs to be treated with caution.

The language forms of story, metaphor, poetry, description, protest, lament, praise etc., taken together with the liturgical forms of sacrament, have the capacity to contain the realities of parallels, contrasts and mystery in ways that enable new tellings of the story to emerge. Indeed, it is worth asking whether a complete understanding about how the Bible relates to the word of God is desirable even if it were possible. To push this further, it is worth asking if a person can really have faith in the God who is revealed in the Bible if they are not in some sense *agnostic*. The opposite of agnostic is gnostic, which means someone who is already fully 'in the know'. If you are fully in the know you don't need faith and you can't make faith claims.

Open Book and Closed Discussion?

The contrast between the nature of the Bible and the formulations of Christian doctrine could not be more marked. Whereas the Bible is made up of a whole bunch of literary forms, doctrine – or rather dogma – consists of closely written, often abstract, theological definitions that are based on tight philosophical analysis and rational argument. The purpose of the Bible is to open up the world of God's speaking and acting amongst the disordered lives of people and nations. The text of the Bible is often ambiguous in its meaning; its truths half-perceived and wide open to interpretation. The purpose of doctrinal statements is to exclude ambiguity and so to reduce the likelihood of wrong belief and practice.

Archbishop Donald Coggan told a story about a church he visited. Everything inside was beautifully ordered, ready for the service to begin. The people knew where they should sit and were all in their places. Outside a howling gale was blowing. Suddenly the doors of the church were blasted open and the wind rushed inside scattering books and papers everywhere. The church leaders managed to wrestle the doors shut and bolt them against the gale, then picked up all of the things that had been scattered around so untidily, making sure everything was just as it had been before. The untidiness caused by the blowing of the wind was to have no place in the ordering and worship of this church. Coggan told this story to challenge the church to welcome the blowing wind of the Holy Spirit that causes theological untidiness even as people are sent out in mission. The picture applies equally well to the popular idea of a contrast between the nature of the Bible and the formulation of doctrine. What the writers of the Bible left untidy and scattered, the Fathers of the church, so this thinking goes, tidied up and put in order.

The simplistic version of this is that after the period of the apostles what Christians believed was in a state of flux, even risking falling into chaos. Then the Fathers of the early church came together in Councils to work out how the preservation of the authentic speaking of God's word in Scripture could lead to the preservation of right belief and right practice in the Church. They produced the statements of orthodox belief that were to be binding on all true Christians for all time. These statements of orthodoxy have come down through the history of the church as the 'catholic' (= universally accepted) Creeds. 'Orthodox' is a combination of two words whose root meanings are about a straight pathway to glory. From time to time new work on the formation of doctrine has been carried out, but essentially these have been designed to call the Church back to its roots in Scripture and the doctrinal formulations established by the mid-fifth century CE. This popular picture is completed when people see the Bible as the foundations, and the doctrines established by the early church as the building constructed on them. But there is a problem here. In a building the superstructure completely obscures the foundation, even though it depends on it for its existence. If the classical formulations of doctrine achieve a high enough profile, they can at least risk obscuring a good deal of what the Bible might have to reveal.

The Bible tends to get read *backwards* through what Christians accept that they are already supposed to believe. Creeds contain no surprises. There are lots of surprises in the Bible. But many of them will remain undiscovered if they are always seen through the lenses of what people think they are already supposed to believe about it. The surprising freshness of the Bible can become like stale bread or old news if the text is not allowed to speak its message without having to get through the filters of prior assumptions about what it is supposed to be talking about. I will return to the relation between the Bible and what Christians believe in the next chapter. Here I will notice some of the pressures that led the early Christians to seek a kind of standardisation in relation to the message of the Bible and the beliefs and behaviours they would hold in common.

'What sort of man is this, that even the winds and the sea obey him?'[12] This exclamation cum question shows as clearly as any text can that the first companions of Jesus had to work out for themselves who he was and what he was doing. The Gospels present their accounts of Jesus' words and actions as fulfilments of scriptural prophecy, but it was far from obvious at first, even to his nearest and dearest, that he could be understood as 'Son of God', 'Messiah', 'Saviour'. The Gospels are thick with questions and confusion from his family and friends as well as from his enemies about who Jesus is, what authority he carries, why he does what he does. The narratives are presented as reflections on experiences that led to the dawning of faith and understanding, not as a series of dogmatic statements that witness to a completed process of such reflection. One of the most obvious omissions from the Gospels, for example, as indeed from the New Testament as a whole, is seen in the absence of any one fully-worked-out doctrine of the atonement being presented as *the* definitive way of interpreting what was going on when Jesus died on the cross. Certainly there are sustained reflections on the call of obedience to the Father's will (John 16—17), language links with Passover (Luke 22:1–23) and sacrifice (John 1:29), and connections between the dying and rising of Jesus and the call to live a holy life (Romans 6:1–11). The most highly-developed reflections on the meaning of Jesus and his suffering are found in the Epistle to the Hebrews' preaching on Jesus as the great high priest, which comes to its climax in Hebrews 10:11–18, and in credal formulae in passages such as 1 Peter 3:18ff. But a neatly-worked-out doctrine that encapsulates all that his death and resurrection is to mean is simply not there.

The sense you get is that the earliest followers of Jesus were still in the process of discovering the significance of what they had experienced and heard. This process was going on at the same time that they were passionately engaged in the tasks of evangelism and mission. As they were crossing cultural and theological boundaries telling and re-telling their stories about Jesus, they came to new depths of understanding what his actions, preaching and suffering were all about. In theological language, it was as they were crossing these boundaries that they began to understand and explore God's purposes and intentions as they had experienced them through Jesus. No passage in the New Testament shows this process taking place more clearly than the story of the conversion of Cornelius, as Peter tells it to the assembled leaders in Acts 11. You can almost hear the penny dropping as realisation dawns in verse 18!

Working out Christian doctrine is about learning to speak the truth about Jesus Christ. As the first Christians moved between political, social and cultural contexts they literally had to face the practical theology questions about how you can talk about Jesus in this new place and still be faithful to him. When they were preaching to fellow Jews they could rely on their shared perceptions of God that were rooted in their common inheritance of Scripture. But when these first Jewish Christians preached among Gentiles, they found themselves doing 'god-talk' among people who were already doing 'god-talk' every day, but with quite different meanings attached to many of the same words. Greek was available as a common language. But as the mission advanced the Christians had to find new accents and languages for their evangelism. Adopting a new language involves learning about new insights that are carried in the grammar and worldviews of that language. This is exactly what you see happening when you watch the transition from Palestinian Jewish Christianity to the Christianity of the Greek-speaking world.

Although the contrast between Hebrew and Greek worldviews that has been part of the mainstream of Christian theology since the nineteenth century has been overblown (because both were very varied within themselves), there is something important to be noticed here. It is this. The great doctrinal confessions of God in creation, incarnation, atonement, salvation and glory; and the foundation doctrine of the Holy Trinity itself were all worked out by churches vigorously engaged in cross-cultural mission. It is easy to lose sight of this lively cross-cultural missionary context. The passion that the Fathers brought to their debates in the early church Councils arose precisely from the fact that the people who came together were reflecting and arguing out of their experience as evangelists, pastors, preachers, politicians. For them, as for many Christians in today's world, their practical theology was literally a matter of life and death. Something of this vigour comes over from the preaching of John Chrysostom on the 'harrowing of hell'.[13]

The great Councils such as Nicea (325 CE) and Chalcedon (451 CE) were intended to establish unity in belief and mission by bringing argument about some key issues to an end. But, unless their doctrinal definitions are understood in the context of vigorous missionary spiritualities, the idea of 'doctrine' regresses into dry and isolated definitions of 'dogma'. For the theologians of the early church 'doctrine' carried the meaning of authentic teaching to be accepted, reflected on, welcomed into prayer, lived out in community. The great doctrinal statements were intended to be the foundational *starting points* for conversation, conversion and discipleship, not just the closing points of abstract arguments. Their aim was that wherever the gospel of Christ was proclaimed it could be guaranteed to be reliably the same message in each place. They were intended to educate Christians about what God is up to and call them to take part in it.

The Creeds used in liturgy consist of short pithy statements and with good reason. In liturgy and pastoral practice creeds have to function not merely as statements of communal solidarity but, also as shared protest and shared testimony, about what it means to stand with others who believe this kind of thing in this kind of world. Dan Hardy, in a discussion about the purpose of theological education of the church's ministers, captures this sense very well: 'The *goal*, I think, is an inhabited Wisdom (immersed in Scripture, the continuity of the Church's life in God, and in a Spirit-informed reason) in the Church, one that is active in responding to the issues of present day life.'[14]

The doctrinal formulations of the early church Councils were part of a missionary conversation that began in Scripture and that continues into the present day. This does not take away from the fact that the outcomes of some of these early Councils were intended to be foundational for all subsequent Christian preaching, spirituality and action. But it does mean that the 'open Bible' and 'open creeds' must be held together in a paradoxical way. They are at the same time both the definitive foundations and also the doors held open as the starting points for Christian mission and theology. The Bible in which God lays his word open to discernment and interpretation by his people holds the priority in this paradox. This intentional openness of the Bible gives the clue to the openness of the process as a whole. Of course, this claim to a shared openness of the Bible and the Creeds leads to another set of questions. If the Bible and the Creeds really are both as foundational and open as I have suggested, might they not be open to new revelations of the purposes of God in the light of new discoveries and new patterns of human behaviour?

Old Word Renewed or New Word Revealed?

Even within the Bible, the question was being raised as to whether some parts of what then counted as Scripture could be laid aside as belonging to a past culture, or whether all parts of the word of God received in the past must remain normative for all time. If some injunctions of Scripture can be seen as time- and culture-specific, can the behaviours that God requires of his people change as cultural norms and contexts change? How could Scripture reveal the word of God in new situations far removed from the settings we find in the Bible? The list of scriptural injunctions that most Christians today consider as no longer binding includes those relating to diet, hairstyles, the death penalty, permission to own slaves, women having leadership roles, borrowing and lending money, etc. It is now widely accepted that Christians can eat what they fancy, drink alcohol in moderation, style their hair as they wish, dress fashionably, refuse to apply the death penalty, outlaw slavery, rejoice in the leadership of women in church and society, and borrow and lend money with suitable safeguards.

However, there are other issues over which people can become bitterly divided. These include homosexuality, which is explicitly forbidden by the Bible; polygamy, which isn't; the slaughter of animals for food, which is simply assumed; the ownership of land and property, on which the Bible is divided; the responsibilities of the wealthy and the priority of care for the poor and the alien, on which it is clear, and the legitimacy of warfare, on which the Bible has no one coherent view. Other issues, such as those related to plant genetics and to human embryology, were not part of the world of the Bible at all, but most Christians assume that the word of the Lord must have something to say about them. These are not merely topics for armchair discussion. They have direct effects on the welfare of millions of people.

Discussions about the authority of the Bible soon develop into debates about how it can be used in relation to ethical issues that require urgent decision and decisive action. The context of this debate has changed radically with the shift in the power-base of the world church from the global north towards the global south that has taken place since the mid-twentieth century. When 'gospel and culture' discussions take place, full engagement with the issues will have to take account of both particular and global contexts within which the Bible is to be received and the word of God is to be heard. This is why seeing the open Bible as the starting point for the conversation about the call of God for the open church as it engages in mission is so important.

Treating the Bible as some kind of literary pope that utters holy truth without regard to circumstance or context will only serve to close some issues that should be left open to the speaking of God.

Simple resort to proof-texting, far from enabling the word of God to be clearly heard, undermines the whole idea of the Bible as revealing the word of God. The very idea of the word or the speaking of God carries the invitation to engage in conversation that can lead somewhere quite new with new resources for getting there. And this gives the clue to the kind of interpretive framework within which the Bible can be set free to offer guidance about God's call to holy living that is expressed in practical action.

All this still leaves open the hard question as to whose interpretation should have priority. Because the possibility of wrong interpretation is ever present, should there be some people or institutions who function as guardians of the truth? To put it bluntly, who owns the Bible?

CHAPTER 3

Who Owns the Bible?

This question is really about who has the right to claim priority for their interpretation, their 'scriptural voice', to be heard. When a person or group claims that their understanding of Scripture should have priority, they are claiming that they are hearing God's word more clearly through Scripture and discerning God's will more closely than other people or groups.

This would not be very important if it was just a matter of gentle disagreement between friends in a home group about the personal spiritual meaning of a text such as, say, Revelation 21:5 ('Behold, I make all things new'), though that could be interesting. But the question of who owns the Bible in the sense of who can rightly claim priority for their interpretation, can be literally a matter of life and death. It has profound implications for the practice of politics, the search for justice, the way groups of people in the same community treat each other, personal and corporate morality, uses and abuses of money and property, and so on.

For example, the Dutch Reformed Church of South Africa's theological sponsorship of apartheid and the theological basis of the mainstream Christian opposition to it were both based on particular interpretations of what the Bible says about the nature of humanity and community. Leaders on both sides of this conflict were firmly committed Christians, but they read their Bibles differently. Because the white minority held the levers of power, their 'ownership' of Scripture counted for more than the readings of people in the black majority. Or consider the way women in Europe were subjugated in relation to their own health, family life, community leadership, access to professions, etc. This had its foundations in biblical patriarchy and in traditionalist interpretations of passages such as Ephesians 5:22 and 1 Corinthians 14:34. Or recall how the use of violence as a way of resolving conflicts between nations found its legitimacy, for Christians who needed such support, from particular interpretations of scriptural text that were used to underpin the theory of just war. Or reflect on how the accumulation of vast wealth by small numbers of powerful people at the expense of the impoverished masses in some of the biggest cities of South America was encouraged among people with strong claims to be Christians, partly because of the failure of the established churches to engage in biblical reflection and challenging interpretation, until the emergence of liberation theologies. By then the problem had become so endemic that only major political intervention could go even a small way to resolving the problems. The role Christian engagement with the Bible might play is a matter for urgent and continuing action and reflection.

Readers might object that all of these examples are cases of questions politics, human rights or economics ask of the Bible rather than questions asked by pastoral practice. But this is a wrong distinction. Systemic racism, gender injustice, violence, poverty and wealth do not exist as theoretical constructs apart from the people and communities who are affected by them. Christian pastoral practice arises from the conviction that God is sufficiently interested in the practical stuff of the world we live in to be involved in its creation, sustenance, healing and its growing in fruitfulness. Christian pastoral practice is about participation in the mission of God in the real world. It involves people being called to the discipline of committed and creative attentiveness to the speaking and action of God. It means reading Scripture positively within the context of the concerns of individuals, families, community groups and nations. This is why the question of who 'owns' the Bible is of key importance.

If the answer is that the Bible is owned by *other* people, far removed from the present context, there is likely to be a series of unspoken assumptions that make relevant local pastoral interpretation of the Bible next door to impossible. Among the most important of these may be that the God of the Bible lives somewhere else, is interested only in what happens somewhere else and can only speak towards my situation abstractly and from a distance. If, however, the ownership of the Bible 'belongs' to the people of God who are called to interpret it in the particular contexts of their actual lives, the assumption is that God is near, interested and involved here and now. I will show later that there are almost as many dangers involved in assuming the second sort of ownership of the Bible as in assuming the first. But for the moment I want to stay with the strategy of locating pastoral practice and the hard question of who owns the Bible in the more local concerns nearer to the working experience of church-based pastoral practitioners. For this I will take us back to the six pictures I offered at the beginning of Chapter 1. In relation to each of them I will raise, but not follow through, some questions that arise about ways of owning the Bible.

- The teenager having her Quiet Time in front of the TV, using her own Bible with the help of her Bible notes, assumes that she has the right to interpret the Scriptures for herself. Her faith and her commitment to hearing God's voice among the other voices that crowd in may well point her in the right direction. But what other resources might she need to ensure that her personal ownership of the Bible will lead her in holy ways rather than becoming a platform for self-assertion expressed in Christian language?
- The cathedral community are owning the Bible as artefact, as symbol, and as vehicle of the speaking of God. But how does this symbolic ownership translate into the kind of practical ownership that can lead to reflection on the *content* of Scripture, such that this community is opened to the challenges it may bring to them? For these people how can the Bible, claimed to be owned by being held up in worship, actually be owned by being translated into active witness?
- David's home-group has a real sense of ownership of the Bible. Through experience they have come to expect that if they faithfully and prayerfully open the Scriptures they will 'hear' God speaking to them directly and personally. They are not surprised that the passage speaks so powerfully to David about his needs. They welcome the renewed openness in the group that his sharing enables among them. But this group has become accustomed to God speaking to them in comforting ways through their shared ownership of the Bible. What strategies might they need to adopt if they are to hear the surprising and disconcerting speaking of God – so that the comfort of owning the Bible can lead to the discomfort of discipleship being renewed?
- Ian and his Bishop are strongly committed to Scripture but they have different ways of owning it. In normal times their presuppositions about how this ownership works are not challenged. The Bishop tends not to be challenged on matters of theology by those around him. Ian preaches his robust sermons to a congregation who already agree with him. The problem comes when Ian and the Bishop have to speak together, outside of their comfort zones, on an issue they both feel passionately about. Ian's view of the Bible as the prescriptive speaking of God and the Bishop's view of the Bible as a much more open book lead them to very different ways of

owning what the Bible says about homosexuality. They are in direct competition for the kind of ownership of the Bible that is most likely to lead to the true speaking of God. How might they find ways of continuing their conversation, and even their relationship as pastor and bishop, when they have such different views about how the Bible is to be owned?

- The people from different faith groups in the airport protest story are all content to own their Scriptures and to allow those Scriptures to guide their thinking and action. But how does the realisation that three different 'Bibles' are involved among these religious communities affect their perception of the Scriptures that are their own? Is God able to speak to anyone who will listen whichever Scriptures they use, and if so will the core message be the same? Are the issues about what owning the Bible might mean in a many-faith context like this too threatening to be engaged with and best left on one side?[1]

- Susan's students are already confident about their ownership of the Bible. She is concerned to help them broaden their understanding of what owning the Bible might mean. Like Ian and the Bishop, they are involved in a kind of power struggle. How might Susan and her students be enabled to hear and explore as fully as possible what well-based ownership of the Bible might mean for them?

Examples of global and local issues that raise the question of who owns the Bible could be multiplied. But there are two problems with the question itself. First we have already seen that the Bible is to be received as an 'open book' that offers a whole range of possibilities for hearing God's voice. People speak about 'using the Bible' a bit like taking tools out of a box. Each tool has its special use, which is to increase the power to get something done. But owning the Bible is not like that. It is simply not that kind of thing.

Second, the word 'own' can carry a range of meanings. The meaning can be legal – I own this house because I have the legal title to it. Or it can carry a psychological meaning – in counselling a client may come to the point of 'owning' that an insight that has emerged describes the reality that they experience. These meanings can be refined. For example, a person may own a property, but they cannot look after it for themselves because they are too young, too old or somewhere else, so decisions about it are taken on their behalf, by trustees. The trustees do not actually own the property, but they have the power to decide how it will be maintained and developed.

Because there is a very close connection between a piece of property and the person who has legal title to it; or between an insight in counselling and the person who accepts it as real for them, 'ownership' carries notions of truth and identity. The truth about what I 'own' to be the case is closely linked to the truth of who I am, the values I hold, the way I act. Because ownership is closely linked to truth and identity, it is also linked to exclusiveness and power. In relation to real estate we use the expression 'property rights', for example, and a whole branch of law is concerned with managing the claims and counter claims that go with this.

The examples above of national and international issues, and of more localised pastoral encounters all contain some level of claimed 'property rights' over Scripture and its interpretation. This highlights a major problem. Claims to ownership of the Bible and therefore to a monopoly on its correct interpretation involve claims by people that their way of seeing things carries the authority of the word of God. The problem is obvious. If different groups are making such claims for different views, whose claims should have priority? One way of solving this dilemma is to allow a free-for-all with everyone having their own view which is to be regarded as equally valid, on the basis of the corporate or individual 'self' as the ultimate authority. But if we hold that the ultimate authority is not the corporate or individual self, but God whose word is revealed through Scripture, there will need to be some way of agreeing how authority to interpret Scripture is to be established. Since God is One, so the argument goes, God's truth must be properly and consistently interpreted. This is why the Church has claimed that God has committed to it trustee authority of the Bible and its interpretation – as a safeguard against the hijacking of Scripture by particular interest groups for their own purposes.

Historically the Church has claimed ownership of the Bible through its monopolies on possession of the text and mediation of its meaning. By maintaining control over the copying of the text; by keeping it in the scholarly language of Latin rather than in the vernacular; and by restricting access to the Bible to approved scholars and duly authorised teachers, the Roman Church was able to exercise virtually unchallenged 'ownership' of the Bible in Western Europe for almost a thousand years. The right 'holding' of the Bible, combined with the right interpretation of the Fathers, the Papacy itself, and the sustained commitment to close association with political and military power, were the unassailable foundations of the authority of the Catholic Church. To be fair, the Church saw itself not so much as the owner of the Bible as its duly appointed guardian. In this role it was exercising the right stewardship of God's word. And Scripture did not stay static. Within the bounds of the monopoly there was vigorous and fruitful theological debate between some of the greatest scholars in Christian history. This often led to fresh interpretations issuing in renewed preaching in relation to (e.g.) the meaning of the cross of Christ, the right appropriation of the sacraments, the refreshment of holy love, spiritual friendship, and much else besides. The tradition of Scripture interpretation was developing, but under strict control.

This monopoly was under challenge well before the Reformation period. The Lollards in the fourteenth century recognised that when control of the Bible is held by those who also hold the levers of intellectual, economic and political power this must lead to Scripture being interpreted to support the interests of the powerful. The spiritual vitality of lay people gave rise to Scripture study-groups in private houses, study circles and devotional guilds that were often associated with the religious orders. In these groups they recognised that they were capable of encountering the word of God without the mediation of the Church. Their encounters with Scripture, so far as it was available, led them to question the right of the Church to dictate to them about the meaning of the Bible. G. R. Evans puts it like this:

> The capacity of heretics to use the Bible for their own ends, notable from the twelfth century, was linked to dissident moves to have Scripture in the vernacular. This was a reflection of the rise of an urban middle class . . . who were articulate and entrepreneurial and did not take kindly to the notion that they must depend upon a priesthood they could see to be poorly educated for their salvation and for the instruction of their souls . . . They were looking to be pilots of their own souls, and to minister to themselves in matters of the Word.[2]

History offers accounts of Christian people being harassed, imprisoned, and even executed by the authorities of the Church on charges of reading and interpreting the Bible. For the Church as the sole guardian of God's word and the sole trustee of God's power on earth, the right ordering of Scripture interpreted within the 'Great Tradition' was the foundation of a rightly ordered, just and godly society. To accept any alternative would be to give way to chaos. Ownership of the Bible and the exercise of power belonged together and power was exercised in the interests of the powerful. By maintaining control over the language and form of the Bible and its interpretation, the Church was in a position to claim the right to declare what God's word demanded about the duties of everybody in Christendom from sovereigns to serfs. Scripture meant what the Church said it meant.

But suppose the boot was on the other foot? Suppose that God wanted to exercise his privilege of ownership of the Church? Suppose that God was minded to call the Church to account for its guardianship of the Bible, or even to use the Bible to criticise the modes of life, worship and mission of the Church? What then? Or suppose that the sovereigns and the serfs and all classes in between were to look somewhere other than the Catholic Church for guidance about God's purposes and God's call? It was questions like these that energised the efforts of the Bible translators and church reformers of the fifteenth and sixteenth centuries. The history of this period has been well explored, so I will not rehearse it here. Suffice to say that the real issue at stake was not simply the missiological and theological question of whether the Bible should be available in the common language, but that the people who were leading this work in parts of northern Europe *were doing so outside of the authority and control structures of the Church.* (There is evidence that vernacular translations of the Vulgate were being produced under the auspices of the Catholic Church as early as the mid-fifteenth century.[3]) The unauthorised translators, interpreters and publishers were taking an axe to the roots of the tree of the Catholic Church's ownership of the Bible.

This all seems a long way from the atmosphere of twenty-first century liberal, democratic societies. But it is important not to dismiss too lightly the medieval Church's concern to guard its monopoly over the Bible. For they recognised only too clearly that if you distance the legitimating authority of the word of God from the authority of the established Church, you cannot avoid the question of how the authority of the Bible and the purity of its interpretation as holy Scripture can be maintained. The authority of the Bible and the authority of the Church and its theological tradition would stand together or would fall separately, and this would affect the stability of Christendom itself.

The Word of God in the Accents of the People

A distinctive fact about the Bible as distinct from the holy books of other world religions, is that the main form of its existence is *as translated text.* The urge to translate the text of Scripture into the languages of the people arises from the determination that the word of God should be made available to all the people of God's world so far as possible in their own languages. Lamin Sanneh reflects on this characteristic of Christianity as from its beginning 'an essentially "translated" religion, linguistically and theologically'.[4] This is evident from Acts, which is essentially a narrative of the translation of the gospel across a series of social and ethnic thresholds. The story of Pentecost (Acts 2:1–11ff) with its question, 'How is it that we hear, each of us, in our own native language . . .?' (v. 8) stands as a kind of manifesto for what follows as the gospel is taken from the heartland of Judaism, via the Jewish Diaspora, to the lands of the Gentiles. At every turn the preachers were faced not only with making their message intelligible and authentic in languages and dialects that were foreign to them, but also with interpreting what the salvation that comes through Christ was to mean in practice in different cultures and contexts.

Translation between languages involves interpretation of the message so that it is both faithful to itself and accessible to the new hearers. For language is a primary vehicle of culture. Transition of preachers between cultures and translation of the message itself is always a matter of cross-cultural interpretation, with all the potential for new revelation and misunderstanding that this involves. We see this process at work in the New Testament. The letters of Paul, for example, are not free-standing theological reflections, but are better understood as responses to situations that arose when the preaching of Christian Jews came face to face with the beliefs and practices of Gentile urban and religious cultures. They are responses to what happens when mission and pastoral practice asks hard questions of the word of God when it is preached. Using 1 Corinthians as an example, we can see that the hard questions there included whether one version of the Christian message is to be preferred in relation to others (chapters 1—4); sexual ethics (chapter 5); the tension between personal freedom and Christian discipline (chapter 6); marriage and divorce (chapter 7); food sacrificed to idols (chapters 8—10); the roles of women in the community of believers (chapters 11 and 14); spiritual gifts and unity in the fellowship (chapters 12—14); the fate of the dead (chapter 15); and charitable giving (chapter 16).

But accepting that Christianity and its Scriptures exist mainly as translated experience and interpreted message means more than simply noting that traditions and practices, and ways of expressing them, vary from place to place. This is significant in itself. But there is a deeper two-way dynamic at work.[5]

1. When Christians accepted that the message could be preached and the Scriptures written in somebody else's mother tongue, they accepted that the new language could be a fit vehicle for the word of God. Because language is the bearer of culture, this also implies accepting that the new culture could in principle be a setting for authentically Christian living. The receiving culture is regarded as a context that is open to the possibility of the speaking of God through the messages of Scripture. It is assumed to be potentially friendly rather than necessarily alien or unholy ground.

2. Second, they committed themselves to a situation where the receiving culture could start asking hard questions about the message of Scripture, such as whether all of it was true for all places and all time; whether some parts of it are more likely to be relevant than others in the new location; or whether it could be relativised according to the needs of the situation. This is exactly what we see happening in the mission narratives in Acts, as I noted in chapter 1. Once it had dawned on the first Jewish Christians that the Gentiles could receive salvation (11:18), they needed to re-think what in their own faith tradition must be retained to maintain its authenticity, and what could be regarded as locally important, but not relevant to the wider context (15:19). Paul's hard-won conclusion that the way to salvation for all people is through faith in Jesus Christ, rather than through fulfilling the requirements of the Jewish law (Romans 1—5) is evidence within the Bible itself of the kind of reflection that had to be undertaken by the first Christian generations. The conversion of Gentiles demanded that Jewish Christians asked hard questions about their own scriptural traditions. The issue at stake was not how Jewish and Gentile Christians could go their separate ways and smile encouragement at one another from a safe cultural distance. It was about how Jewish and Gentile Christians could stand *together as one body* and learn with each other what it means to be people who are saved through Jesus Christ. This involves learning about what it means to be people who have come to share together in the 'ownership' of Scripture.

It is difficult for Christians whose first language is English to appreciate the impact of having the Bible available in one's mother tongue. English is becoming the *lingua franca* for business and media across the world. We have had the Bible available in English for so long that we are no longer surprised by this. But accents as well as languages matter. I remember as a child growing up in the North East of

England in a labouring family, thinking that church and religion must be something to do with posh people from 'down south'. My family and friends all spoke with northern accents, whereas the priests and many of the church people we met spoke with upper class southern accents. The moment I first heard somebody read the Bible and preach with a Geordie accent came as a revelation. The message sounded real and it sounded as if it was for people like us, not just for 'foreigners'.

During my first term at theological seminary in the 1960s a group of us, who all had strong regional accents, were required to take speech lessons so that we could communicate Bible and liturgy in 'the Queen's English'. We found this patronising and alienating, and soon developed strategies to subvert the process. We held that if the Christian message could not be preached in the accents of our homes it could have little relevance to the communities that had given us life. But there is something deeper than this to notice. When you render holy Scripture into a new language, you also render the new language into holy Scripture.

In his discussion of the cultural impact of Scripture in the mother tongues of Russia, Sanneh shows how closely the availability of one's mother tongue for communication of the most significant concerns is related to the dynamics of personal and cultural self-esteem:

> Nicholas Ilminski (1821–91), a brilliant linguist . . . carried the vernacular cause among the Russian Tartars whose language he treated not as a subspecimen of Arabic . . . but as a language in its own right. The story is told of an elderly Tartar who was so struck by the genius of Ilminski's translation that it affirmed the best in his culture. Thus, when he heard devotions in Ilminski's translation he 'fell on his knees . . . and with tears in his eyes thanked God for having vouchsafed to him at least once in his life to pray as he should'. The devout Tartar had been stirred in the depths of blood, soul and tongue. Ilminski illuminated what he called 'the living tongue of the Tartars' *by investing it with scriptural esteem*, so that the popular, everyday language of the people was connected directly to their deepest thought and religious consciousness.[6]

When we read in Acts of the message of Jesus Christ being met with scepticism (17:32–34) or vigorously opposed (19:23ff), this was because it threatened the vested interests of some of the hearers. There is no sense yet that the preaching of the gospel was being misunderstood because it had become linked up with the interests of political or cultural power structures. Indeed, the reverse is the case. The Gospel stories, which were being collected together at the same time as the events described in Acts were taking place, tell of people who would be regarded as outcasts by the rest of society at that time coming to Jesus. People who didn't matter to anybody else mattered a lot to Jesus, and they knew it. People who were lame, blind, mentally or physically ill, lepers, tax collectors, prostitutes, criminals and many more sought him out, hung on his words, received his care, and were transformed by their contact with him. This happened so often that his enemies complained about it (Luke 5:29–32; 15:1–2). The people described as opposing Jesus and his followers in the Gospels and Acts were closely linked up with the religious, economic and political power structures of the time, and this echoes a major theme that runs through the Bible as a whole.

When the first Christians preached their message and translated it across the boundaries of language and culture there was sufficient distance between the proclamation and the power structures of society for the message to be clearly enough heard and have a distinctive appeal to the hearers. Indeed, Paul seems to make a point of the importance of engaging in the work of mission from a position of comparative vulnerability rather than of strength (2 Corinthians 12:9–10). However, as the subsequent history of the Church shows, from the fourth century CE the links between the call to faithfulness to Christ and faithfulness to the powers that be converged, eventually becoming so close that they were hard to distinguish from each other. Far from the Christian message retaining its distinctiveness while being translated so that it could be lived both authentically and attractively across the boundaries between cultures, the sound of the message became so harmonised with the background music of the culture that its distinctiveness was in danger of disappearing. Whereas the Book of Revelation had celebrated: 'The kingdom of the world has become the Kingdom of our Lord and of his Messiah' (11:15), the truth was the other way round – the kingdom of God became identified with the power structures of this world.

This dynamic is important for our question of who owns the Bible. It is one thing to discover that one's language and culture can become a context for celebrating God's word, but it is quite another to discover that welcoming the gospel with its foreign baggage involves rejecting or marginalising one's own culture. Even if missionaries translate the words of their message into words that you recognise, they may fail to translate their message into the 'languages' of your contexts and cultures. The call to believe the gospel can be heard as the call to abandon one's own linguistic and cultural inheritance in favour of that of the preaching invaders. This is the charge levelled at the nineteenth- and early twentieth-century European missionaries to Asia and Africa who arrived with the 'civilising' agenda of empire, importing European values and cultural forms as 'the' ways of being authentically Christian. Missionaries like Hudson Taylor who sought to identify themselves deeply with the new cultures they were meeting risked misunderstanding by their colleagues and rejection by their sponsors.[7] It seems astonishing that as late as the 1970s the idea that serious engagement by missionaries with the new cultures they encountered was still seen as radical. So much so that when Vincent J. Donovan's book on his work with the Masai was published it was regarded as a revelation of a little known missionary method.[8]

This has serious implications for our question of who owns the Bible, for it remains true that in many parts of the world, at the beginning of the third Christian millennium, to be Christian is identified with being from the prosperous north-west. If people from non-Western cultures, or from non-privileged groups within those cultures, are to experience the Bible as belonging to them too, major shifts have to take place in how the messages of the Bible are to be offered, received and understood. To illustrate this I will reflect on the experience of ownership of the Bible among three groups of people who have serious reasons to sense that it could neither belong to them nor speak to them.

African American People and Scripture

Considering the treatment of black people by Christian European whites from the sixteenth century onwards, with the institution of slavery and the expropriation of homelands through conquest and colonisation, it is one of the surprises of history that such large numbers of African and African American people 'own' the Bible in the sense of finding in its stories and teaching firm grounds for personal hope and community transformation.

Vincent Wimbush has explored how the language world of the Bible may have become a 'language-world' for African American Christians.[9] The slavers took steps to separate the Africans they had taken not only from their homelands but also from their languages and religious heritage. '. . . part of what it meant to be fully enslaved was to be cut off from one's cultural roots'.[10] But as part of the process of acquiring new skills, symbols and languages for survival many of the slaves adopted the Bible as a language that told stories of 'heroes and heroines, of heroic peoples and their pathos and victory, sorrow and joy, sojourn and fulfillment . . . the Bible became a "world" into which African Americans could retreat . . . identify with, draw strength from, and in fact manipulate for self affirmation'.[11]

Wimbush traces a pattern of five overlapping 'readings' that have been adopted as African Americans have sought to establish that this book can be 'our book':

1. **Rejection, Suspicion, and Awe of 'Book Religion'.** The first generations of slaves 'could not and did not fail to notice the powerful influence of the Bible upon the Europeans' self-image, culture and orientation'. The notion that religion could be held in a book at all was foreign to the slaves who experienced their own religion in the form of stories, songs, sayings, prayers, movement. The fact that this book was the book that their oppressors held to be holy led to its being regarded with even deeper suspicion. However, argues Wimbush, the fact that this book was appealed to by their captors as the legitimating source for the exercise of power led at least some of the slaves to adapt the stories of the Bible to serve their own needs for affirmation and hope. The first steps were being taken to accepting that the Bible could become 'our book' and not just 'their book'.

2. **Transformation of 'Book Religion' into Religion of Slave Experience.** As the Africans began to convert to Christianity in significant numbers in the eighteenth century in response to evangelical preaching, they began to recognise two things about the Bible – first that it was to be the source of faith and identity, and second that each person had the freedom to interpret the Bible according to their own circumstances and needs.

   They could read certain parts and ignore others. They could and did articulate their interpretations in their own way . . . by the end of the century the Bible had become a virtual language-world that they too could enter and manipulate in light of their social experiences. After all, everyone could interpret the Bible under the guidance of the Spirit, that is, in his or her own way.[12]

   This meant drawing on the stories of Scripture, especially those that testified to hope and freedom in the face of bondage, as providing

the ground and resonance for stories, testimonies, sermons, exhor-
tations, songs. 'Interpretation was . . . controlled by the freeing
of the collective consciousness and imagination of the African
slaves as they heard the biblical stories and retold them to reflect
their actual social situation, as well as their visions for something
different.'[13]

If Wimbush is right, what we see at work is a process of appropriating the ownership of Scripture through recognising that the
stories in the Bible resonate with the experiences of the story tellers,
song singers, preachers and pray-ers in the here and now. In short,
ownership of the Bible arises out of an acceptance that the God of
the Bible and the people of the Bible presently inhabit the same
world as the new readers.

3. **Establishment of Canon and Hermeneutical Principle.** Around
the time of the American Civil War a wider range of the Bible text
was being engaged with. Attention was given to Old Testament
writings about social justice, right treatment of the poor and the call
to recognise all men as brothers created in the image of God. Close
attention was given in preaching to biblical models, such as the
Promised Land as where people live now, not just after death; the
challenge to institutional racism; and to New Testament texts such
as Galatians 3:28. Here more of the Bible is being owned for a
greater range of purposes, including the call to considered and systematic opposition to the state of things as they are. In this 'reading'
the God of the Bible is openly characterised as taking the side of the
enslaved and calling for a just society.

Wimbush quotes the preaching of Frederick Douglass (1845): 'the
overwhelming mass of professed Christians of America . . . would
be shocked at the proposition of fellowshipping a sheep stealer; and
at the same time they hug to their communion a man-stealer and
brand me an infidel if I find fault with them for it'.[14] The 'prophetic
apology' of this kind of 'reading' is used in pursuit of justice for all
in a society characterised by reconciliation of each with all under
the banner of Scripture which belongs to the whole nation. This
approach was strongly echoed late in the twentieth century in
South Africa in Archbishop Desmond Tutu's April 1988 letter to
State President Botha, in which on the basis of a wide-ranging biblical argument he declares: '. . . your apartheid policies are not only
unjust and oppressive. They are positively unbiblical, unchristian,
immoral and evil.'[15]

4. **Esoteric and Elitist Hermeneutical Principles and Texts.** People

who gave up hope of full integration into society began to seek new hope in closer, more exclusive groups that claim 'exclusive knowledge of other holy books, or previously apocryphal parts of the Bible; and to practice bibliomancy (the reading of holy books for the purpose of solving personal problems or in order to effect some wonder from which one can benefit').[16] This 'reading' depends on esoteric ways of relating to the holy books that are used. The standards of the wider society are rejected; the methods of Bible interpretation used by mainstream Christian groups are rejected; what is 'owned' are ways of relating to what is held to count as Scripture that will strengthen the identity and purposes of a closed group. The focus tends to be on literal interpretation of mythological parts of the Bible.[17] Groups who feel under threat draw their boundaries of belief and practice and use their 'ownership' of the Bible to reinforce their solidarity and focus their future hope.

5. **Fundamentalism (Late Twentieth Century).** Wimbush comments on the large numbers of African Americans being attracted to white fundamentalist communities. The aim is to 'secure the "fundamentals" of the faith against the inroads of "modernism"'. The quest is for a reliable community of safety that gives a strong sense of identity, belonging and purpose and a secure set of allegiances to support the proclamation of the values of the group. The key difference between the previous reading and this one is that while the former seeks salvation through isolation from the surrounding culture, this group retains a universalising perspective. What is true for this group *ought* to be true for the rest of the world. If everyone else owned the Bible to be as we own it to be . . .

These five African American 'readings' or ways of 'owning' the Bible all find their energy from an orientation of faith, the pressure of personal and community circumstances, and the conviction that if the Bible does reveal the word of God, the state of things as they are should be different and better. The linkage between experiences of personal and communal powerlessness and different ways of using the Bible to legitimate particular kinds of action is clear. In other words, how you read the Bible depends a lot on where you read it, your circumstances when you read it and who you read it with. If a person's or a community's circumstances place them in a position where they are pushed around by the powers that be in society and/or the Church, they have only three choices.

1. They can accept the standard 'readings' but, recognising themselves as not fitting in, keep silent about their sense of alienation.
   This choice involves acknowledging that the Bible is owned not by
   them, but by more powerful people to whom they are permanently
   indebted for allowing some kind of left-over relationship to
   Scripture.
2. They can try to find their own voices to offer their alternative 'readings' into the faith conversation, in the hope that the story of
   Scripture might be able to be told, at least to them and their kind, in
   their own languages and their accents.
3. They can give up the enterprise altogether, convinced that however
   hard they try, there is no way that they will ever be able to 'own'
   that the Bible is about them and for them.

Women and Scripture

The first option, inherited by generations of women, accepts that traditional interpretations of Scripture by male preachers and theologians carry the authority of God. You can't argue with 'God' and win.
So many women accept, for example, Paul's teaching in 1 Corinthians
11:1–16 which connects the status of women with the divine hierarchy
('I want you to understand that Christ is the head of every man, and
the husband is head of his wife, and God is the head of Christ' [v. 3])
as the reason why women should take second place to men in worship and prayer. Many women continue to accept that the teaching of
Ephesians 5:22–23 ('Wives, be subject to your husbands as you are to
the Lord. For the husband is head of the wife just as Christ is the head
of the church . . .') legitimates their exclusion from church leadership
and ordained ministry. These are examples of interpretation of biblical texts without regard for the sociological context in which they
were written or the present contexts within which they can be read.
They have the effect of making women subservient to men while
claiming that this is God's will. The point is that women who accept
that priority in ownership of the Bible belongs to their menfolk are
likely have their identity, their beliefs and their behaviour dictated by
men. Any ownership of the Bible they have will be second-hand. The
Bible will speak God's word to them, but other people will tell them
the terms and conditions of that speaking.

The second option arises from the conviction that when women discover that their own voices and accents not only can, but must be
used as media for interpreting the Bible, they carry the sounds of the
refreshing and true speaking of God through Scripture. This involves

a real liberation of the Bible. New interpretations of familiar parts of the Bible are offered. Sections of the Bible that have remained unnoticed or only lightly regarded for centuries are brought into the open. Nor is it only that the half-noticed, unnoticed and silent women of the Bible have been allowed to speak for themselves for the first time. There is much more to the feminist liberation of Scripture than just listing and interpreting all the references to women in the Bible. The feminine resonances of so much of biblical language about God, the nature of covenant relationships and the nature and values of God's people are also made visible. This has become possible because of the hard questions that the experiences of women have put to the Bible. Kathleen Fischer asks:

> How can women relate to writings that are the product of a patriarchal culture, writings which function as the final appeal in claims for male superiority and the subordinate role of women? Can the Bible still be the word of God for us? Can we turn to Scripture as a resource for prayer?[18]

She identified four possibilities that are opened up for women as a result of the work of feminist theologians. These are 'discovering ourselves in the stories of biblical women'; 'finding hope in liberating Scripture passages'; 'remembering and mourning women's pain', 'listening to the Bible's silences'.[19] These possibilities are major parts of the agenda of what it might mean for women to be able to 'own' the Bible.

Fischer was working in the field of spiritual direction and was encouraged in her engagement with some of the really tough passages of the Bible by the seminal work of the American Bible scholar Phyllis Trible. Trible's study of four of the forgotten women of the Old Testament has become a classic.[20] Her study combines careful analysis of the stories of Hagar, Tamar, the unnamed woman in Judges 19 and the Daughter of Jephtha. She identifies the alienation and pain of these suffering women with the agonies of Christ echoed in Christian interpretations of Isaiah 53: [Hagar] 'is bruised for the iniquities of Sarah and Abraham; upon her is the chastisement that makes them whole'.[21] Tamar is 'a woman of sorrows and acquainted with grief'.[22] The unnamed woman's 'body was broken and given to many'.[23] In meditating on Jephtha's daughter the writer cries out, 'My God, my God, why hast thou forsaken her?'[24] Trible's theological method as she reclaims ownership for women of these biblical stories is provocative as well as distinctive in interweaving textual analysis, meditation with a variety of symbols resonating together and poetic prayer. But the distinctive thing about it is that she allows the Bible text to speak for itself – with its feminine voices and with the accents of particular women.

There can be a tendency to ransack the Bible and Christian tradition to make them say what we want them to mean. This is as true about feminist interpretation of the Bible as about other issues. Re-creating Scripture in our own image is just as likely to lead to further oppression as deliberately or accidentally restricting its ownership in the first place. That is why it is important to engage in the painstaking work of critical study of the text as well as appropriating or owning it for our own purposes. A good example of this process at work in partnership with major streams of Christian tradition and sustained reflection on the relationship between women, Christ and the Bible is by Rosemary Radford Ruether, who refuses to engage in simplistic interpretations of texts like Galatians 3:28, however congenial they may appear to be to the feminist cause. For her and for most women theologians becoming 'owners' of the Bible does not come cheap.[25]

For some the cost is not worth paying. In the UK, the theologian and philosopher Daphne Hampson[26] has taken the third option, describing herself as 'post-Christian' and holding that because of its oppressive patriarchal dynamics and the dubious nature of its truth claims, based on the ways the Bible has been used, Christianity can no longer be regarded as either true or moral. Hampson's approach is much more than someone throwing up their hands in despair because they find some of the stories in the Bible about women too hard to stomach. Hers is a carefully considered approach borne out of careful philosophical and ethical reflection about a wider range of matters than the Bible's approach to gender awareness. She considers the Bible's witness to the religious experiences of people and their claims about an exclusive, excluding, and partisan God as functionally irrelevant to the world at the turn of the third millennium. She also finds the ethical frameworks of the Bible and its privatisation to the interests of the Churches morally indefensible in the face of the many faith and multi-cultural societies of the post-modern world, each of whom have legitimate cause for their truth claims to be heard and evaluated.

There isn't space here to consider Hampson's approach in any detail, but there is something important that Christians need to consider carefully as they seek to own and interpret the Bible. Christians have become so used to seeing the Bible through the lenses of their own interests, the Church's teaching and the basic standards of European 'civilised' societies that they find it very difficult to engage with the kind of critique of the Bible that people like Hampson set out. The hard questions that pastoral practice asks of the Bible cannot just be spiritualised away as if the message of Scripture must automatically be good news for everybody, for no other reason than that it *is* Scripture.

As Phyllis Trible showed in *Texts of Terror*, over-traditional, over-spiritualised, cheap and easy engagement with Scripture will not do. There has to be careful engagement with the text that connects the resources of analytical skills, pastorally sensitive imagination, hospitable spiritual awareness and courage to argue with the messages that it offers. If the Bible is to respond to the hard questions pastoral practice asks, it must be allowed its 'wildness', so that the immense untidiness of Scripture can encounter the messiness and disorder that are as characteristic of human experience now as they were of human experience when its books were being written.

'Non-religious' People and Scripture
Uncomfortable Insiders
'Uncomfortable insiders' attend public worship and take part in church teaching and fellowship groups; but for them the voices of the Bible are incapable of speaking in their own languages and accents. This group includes many lay people and even clergy who are active, but often uncomfortable, in the life of the Church. To be 'religious' in this sense is to be in the driving seat as far as other people's religious experience is concerned. To be 'non-religious' is to be powerless and needing to keep to yourself the truth about who you are and what you believe.

Examples include people 'from the wrong side of the tracks' in churches where the dominant culture is professional, successful, competitive; gay people in churches where the preaching is strongly anti-gay; people who have questions and doubts in churches where there is a strong emphasis on confidently knowing and testifying to your faith; clergy in evangelical churches whose faith has grown in new directions, but whose congregations continue to expect them to 'tell me the old, old story'. Here pastoral experience asks how you can 'own' a Bible that is genuinely open to further interpretation, new exploration and fresh discovery, in a church that has largely domesticated it to reflect the dominant faith-style of the congregation, and in which people who are different have to keep quiet about themselves for fear of rejection.

Jenny Richardson tells her story about some Christians living in a high-rise block in Sheffield where lifts were broken, vandalism was rife, tradespeople refused to visit, and the local council had installed an incinerator that spewed out pollution nearby. They soon found themselves wanting to interpret the Bible as a resource for social action, not just as the groundwork of personal spirituality, which had previously been their normal approach. The important thing about this story is that it not only represents a shift in Jenny's theology of understanding herself and her community; but that it challenged the local church as a whole to move out of its comfort zone and re-examine how Scripture could be interpreted to resource decisions about right action in their inner urban context. She comments:

> This question about processes [of interpretation] needs to be asked of those who use the Bible in the urban areas of Britain. Those who are responsible for theological education with the urban laity are faced with a choice between imposing theological understanding or offering their specialist biblical knowledge to enable local people to do their own theology – and perhaps come to some surprising conclusions.[27]

Uncomfortable Outsiders

These are people who belong to organizations that are associated with churches, and who relate to those churches by sharing with them in community service of various sorts. Examples might include governors of church schools who are not themselves practising Christians; a lunch club for the elderly run in a church hall by a mixed group of people from the host church and the wider community; a youth club started by Christians and meeting on church premises and that is now run by local authority sponsored leaders; a soccer team that started with a church choir and that now belongs to a Sunday morning league. These people are 'non-religious' not in the sense that they have no faith or spirituality, but in the sense that they often have to work with norms that the churches they are associated with stand for, but that they may not themselves share. The reason for including this group is that these are all contexts where boundary conflicts of various sorts commonly arise. They present as being about who is allowed to use church-owned premises for what kind of purpose; or whether a community group can be allowed to use the name of the church (St Mary's Dancing School, All Saints Football Club, etc.) when they have little other allegiance to the church. Not far under the surface in such local turf wars lie conflicts of ownership of resources and of values about how such ownership is to be worked out.

There can be parallels between how a local church treats its 'ownership' of the Bible and the way it relates to partnership opportunities with the local community. A church that sees itself as the guardian of the truth of Scripture and that has conservative and clearly understood (at least by its leaders) standards of exegesis of Scripture is likely also to have a clear sense of boundary between itself and the local community. It is likely to see partnerships with the local community as having at least an implicit evangelistic purpose. A church with a more open approach to the Bible and its interpretation is likely to have a more open attitude to partnerships in the local community that can show itself in some shared values that can lead to shared action. This may be no more than to say that an openness towards the ownership of the Bible is likely to reflect a more general openness. The point I am making is that the way pastoral encounters between church and community groups working in partnership or in competition with each other are handled may be a significant indicator of how that church relates to its core values, and therefore how in its particular context it 'owns' the Bible.

Professional Outsiders

A third group of 'non-religious' people might, paradoxically, be people who are experts in religious knowledge of various sorts, but whose engagement with the Bible is, as a matter of principle, from outside the community of faith. Examples could include teachers of religious studies in state schools, colleges and universities and even some professors of theology. The common factor here is that the Bible, its teaching, its history and its place in present-day society are understood phenomenologically, as something to be examined that must in principle to be kept separate from the personal spirituality and convictions of the teachers and their students. The religious practices of people, whether Christians, Muslims, Hindus or Bahai, and their engagement with their Scriptures are described and explored in terms of social anthropology, linguistics, ethical theory, psychology of religion, etc. The assumption, where Christianity is being examined, is that the Bible is a universal inheritance that can properly be owned and explored by anybody who cares to do so. This is not a very different to the approach taken by dramatists, film makers and authors who take the stories of the Bible and adapt them for their own purposes. In this sense the Bible is public property, available to be owned and used by everybody, and vulnerable to the uses and abuses that come with this. Certainly teachers and scholars will be careful to act with integrity so that their explorations are as well-directed and well-founded as possible. The dramatists and film makers may choose to exercise no such discretion. The similarity between them is that both the religious studies scholars and the dramatists depend for their success on appropriating the ownership of the Bible for their purposes, and on distancing the text of the Bible from the spiritualities of the churches and communities that have traditionally claimed to own it. In other words, they depend on being able to treat the Bible as public and open text like any other text, rather than as holy Scripture.

The results of claiming the ownership of the Bible for everybody by scholars can be very creative, but they can also miss the point entirely as a result of the separation of the interpretation of the Bible from a commitment to a life of prayer and right action. I think this is less often the case when dramatists, artists and film makers claim the right to interpret the Bible as they wish, because often their creativity is aimed at probing into the meanings of things. When the results cause established Christians to howl with protest at the interpretations that arise, there is a kind of confrontation between the Bible text as it stands and the presuppositions of the churches who see themselves as its guardian, if not as its owner. Where this confrontation or this new opening of the Bible to the shining-in of a different light leads to passionate argument, considered dialogue or renewing of basic questions, it seems to me that the Bible discloses its openness for everyone and its unwillingness finally to be owned by anyone.

Facing the question of who owns the Bible reveals what we might call its vulnerability and awkwardness. Perhaps these come as close as we have been able to get so far to suggesting what kind of relationship there might be between the Bible and the word of God. For in choosing to speak at all, God chooses to disclose his presence, his love, his purposes to people. In living with the results of what the writers of the Bible and the compilers of the Canon have assembled, God becomes utterly vulnerable to whatever the writers and readers and hearers and interpreters of the Bible make of these times of speaking, hearing and arguing back. Through it all, the Bible stands in its givenness. It is in this givenness that the essential awkwardness of the Bible is found. That is why when the Bible and pastoral practice meet, hard questions are bound to be asked from both sides.

CHAPTER 4

How Does the Bible Witness to Jesus Christ?

Expected Words

The girl reading her Bible in front of the TV wears a wristband bearing the letters 'WWJD'. Her friends at church have WWJD stickers and badges to remind them to keep asking, 'What would Jesus do?' They assume that they can know what Jesus would do in a variety of challenging situations, including many not found in the Bible. They assume there is a bond between the mind of the Christian and the mind of Jesus. Jesus is seen as a friend (as well as Lord) whose will can be clearly known, acted on and taught to other people.

All six pictures of the Bible being used contain this assumption. The cathedral congregation experience the gospel book as a familiar symbol surrounded by other familiar symbols. Because for them the words of Jesus come as *expected* words the challenges they contain can easily be masked or even lost. The home group also experiences the Bible as expected words. They tend to choose passages to read that affirm them in the culture of their faith and commitments. Ian and his Bishop are both clear about what the Bible teaches and their knowledge of the Bible has formed the views they hold. Their expectations of what the Bible teaches are already set: Scripture can spring no surprises on them. The group affected by the airport development are in principle more open to the surprises that the Bible may spring on them because the questions they bring to their reading of Scripture about the airport issue are unfamiliar ones for them. But their responses to the Bible are still likely to be conditioned by their inherited patterns of hearing and reading it, as well as by their defensiveness about the huge developments that will affect their communities. They too will tend to seek the support of expected words. Susan's students also experience the Bible as expected words. She is keen to introduce her class to the puzzling and surprising nature of Scripture and its interpretation, but they already know 'what Jesus would do'.

This sense, that Jesus' words come to his people as expected words, is understandable as far as it goes. The very existence of present-day Christian churches is built on the assumption that the purposes of Jesus and those of present-day Christians go basically with the grain rather than against it. Even when they do experience Jesus' teaching as cutting across the grain of their experiences and intentions, Christians tend to hear this as the call of a familiar Christ to renewed faithfulness in relation to familiar actions and attitudes, rather than the call of a stranger to move away from home ground into foreign and disturbing territory. Christians too easily assume that the Jesus of the Gospels is 'one of us' – that Jesus was himself a Christian and that the Bible in general and the New Testament Gospels in particular are Christian books. In an important sense they are. But it is not a very big step from making this assumption uncritically to seeing the Gospels as essentially churchy rather than missionary documents, and interpreting them in ways calculated to underpin the particular values of Christian groups and of institutional churches.

Certainly, if we use a basic surface reading of the Gospels, there is evidence of a continuity of interest between Jesus and the people he meets. The calling of the first disciples (Mark 1:16f) presupposes that there had been contact before this time between Jesus and these men. The references to Jesus being 'at home' (Mark 2:1 and 3:19) suggest there was some community he lived amongst in the early days of his public ministry. There are frequent references to large crowds coming to hear him (e.g. Luke 8:4; 12:41). His entry into Jerusalem on a donkey had clearly involved advance preparation by friends or supporters (Luke 11:1ff). His closest disciples are moved by the messianic hopes he inspired in them, even if they grasp the wrong end of the stick (Mark 10:35). His teaching and example command passionate declarations of loyalty (Matthew 26:35). In John Jesus speaks of his disciples as his 'friends', in the special sense of the ones who not only recognise his key values, but who are committed to living them out (John 15:12ff). Almost throughout the Gospels we are given the sense that his disciples are in community with Jesus. They hear his call and follow him where he leads – well, almost. There is plenty of evidence in the New Testament of continuity between the concerns, hopes and commitments of Jesus and those of his disciples.

Unexpected Words

But there is also plenty of evidence of discontinuity – and much of this concerns what is unique, surprising, strange, and ultimately disturbing about Jesus and his message. The balance definitely lies in this direction – the Gospels seem to go out of their way to highlight the essential otherness and strangeness of Jesus. From the birth narratives in Matthew and Luke to his death between two criminals Jesus moves through the Gospels as the one person who really knows what is going on, but also as somehow a stranger to everybody, including his own immediate family. He is portrayed as confronting the forces of evil in people (Mark 1:23); healing people from physical and spiritual sickness (Mark 2:1–12); taking authority against a storm (Mark 4:35f). He is in frequent confrontation with the spiritual leaders of the communities he visits and this comes to a head in his pre-meditated acted parable of 'cleansing the temple' (Mark 11:17). The picture of Jesus as the friend who is ultimately a stranger even to his closest disciples is at its sharpest in Matthew's presentation of Peter's response to Jesus question, 'Who do people say that I am?' (Matthew 16:13–23). Here we witness the clearest match between the identity and purpose of Jesus and his disciples, but it is quickly followed by Jesus' clearest rejection of their understanding of him. 'But he turned and said to Peter, "Get behind me, Satan! You are a stumbling block to me; for you are setting your mind not on divine things but on human things"' (v. 23). Indeed, the places in the Gospels where Jesus appears to be most 'at home' is when he is with 'tax collectors and sinners' (e.g. Mark 2:15; Luke 15:1ff). There are hints here of the kinds of community of purpose that present-day pastoral practitioners may share with Jesus. Marginalised and sinful people are clearly on the agenda of both. But the essential strangeness of Jesus should lead us to be cautious of making over-easy connections.

The Jesus we meet in the Gospels is very different from the familiar friend speaking expected words that reinforce the kinds of personal identity, community spirituality, and active discipleship that we see in our six pictures of people using the Bible. Not only is he often strange to his family and friends, but he is also in clear opposition to the religious leaders who in their own terms know exactly 'what Messiah would do'. As far as they are concerned he wouldn't do what Jesus does. I suggest that when we begin to recognise in the New Testament witness to Jesus the stranger who is somehow *for* his people, we open up the possibility that present-day pastoral practice and Jesus might have something to say to each other, even if this something takes the forms of hard questions. As the stranger he called his hearers to a new way of being friends not only with each other, but with God. Through Jesus the first believers heard themselves being called to befriend not only strangers within their own communities, but also Gentiles and even their enemies. The call Matthew presents as Jesus 'famous last words' to his disciples is the call to 'Go and make disciples of all nations . . .' – to take his message far beyond God's chosen people Israel (Matthew 28:19). This understanding of Jesus as friend of sinners, stranger to the righteous, and the one who sends his follower to move beyond the boundaries of their own accustomed experience should serve as a severe warning to twenty-first century Christians that when it comes to a choice between the world as it is and the churches as they are, Jesus may not always side with the churches as his first choice option.

Shared Words

So what might be the prospects of establishing a creative conversation between Jesus as he is presented in the New Testament Gospels and present-day pastoral practice? Even if it is accepted that Jesus is as likely to be encountered as stranger as he is as friend, there are dynamics at work that can serve to make getting this conversation going at least problematic. These dynamics concern the nature of the Gospels themselves and the nature of pastoral practice.

The historical background, literary structure and theological interpretation of the Gospels continue to be the subject of wide-ranging investigation and this is not the place to present a survey of the major studies.[1] For present purposes it is enough to note five things about the Gospels as they are presented.[2]

1. The Gospels Are Episodic

Some sections of the Gospels consist of very short episodes presenting Jesus as first meeting one group of people, then another, then another; speaking in short confrontational protests; telling parable stories; asking sharp questions, but almost never presenting doctrinal discourses. Take the first couple of chapters of Mark. The text moves almost without explanation from the banks of the River Jordan, to the 'wilderness', to the shores of Galilee. The encounters include the baptism of Jesus, the call of the first disciples, the healing in a synagogue of 'a man with an unclean spirit', the healing of Peter's mother-in-law, healings of people brought to the house, travels around Galilee, cleansing a leper, healing a paralysed man, eating with tax collectors and sinners, teaching about feasting and fasting, and a confrontation about the meaning of the Sabbath – all in just over 50 verses. At other times the episodes are more protracted, such as the sayings grouped in the 'Sermon on the Mount' in Matthew 5—7; or teaching about the age to come, presented in Matthew 23–25.

John is also presented episodically, though here we do find a smaller number of collections of sayings delivered as more fully presented episodes, such as the 'farewell discourses' and Jesus' 'high priestly prayer' in chapters 14—17. Matthew and Luke present the birth narratives as a series of short episodes that contain visitations, sayings and encounters by a rich mixture of heavenly, earthly, powerful and powerless, holy and unholy characters. All four Gospels present the passion and resurrection narratives as sequences of episodes involving a bewildering array of individuals who are caught up in the action, with only Jesus himself seeming to have some sense of what was really happening. As the Gospels move quickly in groups of disjointed or more joined-up episodes, they seem to me to have more in common with twenty-first century television soap operas than with extended theological or doctrinal discourses.

2. The Gospels Are Carefully Structured

In a TV soap several story lines run at the same time, each in short clips of action, with the characters speaking in parts of sentences more often than making long speeches. The things the characters say have superficial meaning for some, but carry a much greater impact for others who are more 'in the know' about that part of the story line. The stories in a particular soap tend to move in parallel. Then like railway lines they arrive at crossover points where they all come together in a confusing pattern, then move forward and follow their own journeys again for a time. Another feature of TV soaps is important. They are screened, not only several times a week but sometimes several times in one evening. The idea is for viewers to get caught up as participants in the matrix of ongoing stories, identifying with the characters, allowing the viewers' own stories to resonate with the on-screen story. This is highly successful in promoting 'brand loyalty' as we see when actors who portray soap characters are not only used to advertise products, but also receive wedding presents, condolence cards, hate mail, etc. on behalf of the characters they portray.

Like stories in the television soaps, the episodic stories in the Gospels are designed to call the hearers, watchers and readers into communities of involvement, curiosity and commitment. Only very rarely in soaps are the viewers told 'what the story means' – they are simply presented with the action and left to interpret it for themselves. Although there is a fair amount of 'what the story means' in John's Gospel – the 'I am' sayings, for example – much of what Jesus says is deliberately allusive rather than explicit or expository, as we see when the disciples are shown as frustrated or puzzled (e.g. John 16:16–18ff). There is a real sense in which the people listening in on the gospel stories are left to set out on their own interpretive journeys – to discover for themselves what Jesus is saying, to find out for themselves 'what Jesus would do'.

The Gospels are presented episodically, but the episodes are not presented randomly, any more than TV soaps are presented randomly. The materials in all four Gospels are grouped together in ways that express the intentions of the writers and later editors. Examples include the way 'lost and saved' parables are grouped in Luke 15—16; teachings about kingdom and judgement in Matthew 23—25; the way each of the passion and resurrection narratives themselves are differently presented. The Gospels focus on 'the story of Jesus', in particular ways that call for the response of faith and commitment. In this sense the structure and purpose of the Gospels are quite different from those of TV soaps. TV soaps are designed to tell a never-ending story that sustains the loyalty of viewers for years at a time, and so provides a secure vehicle for advertising revenue. The Gospels are designed to present stories that happened 'once for all', so that the hearers are brought to make up their minds about Jesus. In soaps you watch the story and make up your mind, without realising it, about what is being advertised – what is *not* in the story. In the Gospels you make up your mind about Jesus, who is at the centre of the story itself.

All four Gospels lead to the same point, though in different ways. This is the point where Jesus of Nazareth, who has lived among his people; called a community together to be bearers of his message; suffered, died and been buried, is encountered alive from the dead and sending his followers to witness to the coming of his kingdom before the world. The question is always hovering around as to who Jesus actually is, for he is clearly so much more than just the man from Nazareth. At times the question is explicit. 'Who can forgive sins, but God alone?' (Mark 2:7); 'Who do you say that I am' (Matthew 16:15); 'Who then is this, that he commands even the winds and the water and they obey him?' (Luke 8:27); 'Surely the Messiah does not come from Galilee, does he?' (John 7:41). But the answer to the question is mostly left open – those who receive the gospel have to make up their own minds who they think Jesus is and what they think Jesus would have them do. This clearly knowable and yet partly hidden Jesus is the one who issues the call, 'Follow me.' In the Gospels there is always this combination of clarity and mystery that requires the people who meet Jesus to look more closely, listen more carefully and make up their minds more fully, not so much about who he is, but about who he is for them.

3. The Gospels Leave a Lot Unexplained

All four Gospels present stories of individuals coming to Jesus or being brought to him desperately ill, oppressed by demons, even having died. Others come with searching questions because they really are seeking to live according to God's purposes or because they want to nail Jesus with their prejudices. People come into contact with Jesus, are healed or called or confronted in some way that changes them, then they disappear and the story moves on, leaving a trail of unresolved loose ends. Jesus himself, the disciples he calls, especially the twelve, some members of his own family and friends and his opponents continue through all the episodes. Otherwise people come onto the scene, encounter Jesus, and go away again leaving hanging in the air the questions about what happened to them later. Did the paralysed man let down through the roof get a job afterwards? What happened when the Gerasene demoniac got home? Did Zacchaeus actually pay up? How many headaches were around after the excessive drinking at the wedding in Cana of Galilee? Did blind Bartimaeus have good eyesight right into old age? What happened to Jesus' mother in later life?

Questions like these can seem trivial, anachronistic, irrelevant, but they highlight the issue that if the Gospels are not about real people and about a real Jesus they are no more than detached pious or mythical texts from the past. In relation to our question of how the witness of the Gospels to Jesus can relate to present-day Christian pastoral practice they are very important as we will see later when we look at the nature of pastoral practice.

4. The Gospels Are 'Located' in the Worship and Mission of Communities of Witness

The Gospels were not written mainly to be read quietly as devotional texts, but to be spoken in communities. They were most probably written to preserve the authentic witness of the first generations of

Jesus' followers at a time when they were coming to the ends of their lives. The Gospels were compiled by people who staked their lives on their experience of the risen Christ among them. They were committed to his teaching and energised by the Holy Spirit, which they interpreted as God's life within them. They were rooted in their local contexts, and determined to bear their witness to Christ and the kingdom of God however costly that might be. They had not read the whole story they were telling in its theological and historical contexts before they took part in it. So right from the beginning they were committed to the process of discovering from their experience exactly who Jesus was for them and just what kind of living witness he was calling them to. In short, they were involved in processes of living and interpreting practical theology as participants in the mission of Christ.

The questions of Jesus' followers about who he was and what he was for needed to be put to their present experience in the later parts of the first century CE with a sense of urgency. They were questions, the answers to which would lead them to make judgements about what Jesus would have them do, what they should teach, how they should pray, how they could support one another and live together with their differences, whether he was worth dying for in the face of persecution. Facing such questions meant being committed to costly living with the answers that emerged, even to the laying down of life if necessary. The people asking these questions as they were seeking to bear their authentic witness to the life and message of Christ lived in learning communities of spirituality, commitment, action and reflection. To summarise, when pastoral practice asks hard questions of Jesus as the Gospels witness to him it is addressing them to texts that are themselves the direct products of pastoral practice facing hard questions.

5. The Gospels Express and Reinforce Practical Theological Commitments of 'Christian Discipleship'

The Christian story is rooted in faith . . . that when the Christian story has been told, a story with themes of preparation and incarnation, of crucifixion and resurrection, of ascension and the coming of the Spirit, *even then the whole story has not been told.* As the story has a beginning, even so it shall have an ending.'[3]

But you can't know the 'end' without taking part in the story. Although the Gospels of Matthew, Luke and John have carefully worked endings, they are all clearly incomplete in the sense of being far from 'the whole story of Jesus'. The final sequences of all four Gospels, even the relatively clumsy endings of Mark, point forward and invite the hearer to take part in 'what happens' next. In the case of John this is explicit, '. . . but these are written so that you may come to believe that Jesus is the Messiah, the Son of God, and that through believing you may have life in his name'(John 19:31).

We can put it like this. The purpose of the Gospels is to establish that the sure foundations for living hope-fully with God in the world are grounded in the story of Jesus the man from Nazareth, whom his followers come to believe is no less than God with them, for them, within them. In Jesus God is with them because he shares their humanity – all of it, even to the point of death and beyond. In Jesus God is for them because he speaks directly to the realities they live with every day. Through the Holy Spirit Jesus is God within them bringing forth transformations of identity, confidence and purpose. I said earlier that the endings of the Gospels serve as invitations to take part in 'what happens next'. From beginning to end, the Gospels are stories-with-a-purpose. The purpose is that their stories become 'our story'.

There is a world of difference between taking an active part in a story and just watching it as a spectator. I once went with a group of friends to a performance of Shakespeare's *Julius Caesar*. When we arrived some of us were given pink tickets and the others were given blue ones. The blue ticket holders were conducted straight to the auditorium which was set out 'in the round', while the rest of us were taken to an adjoining hall where we were plied with free drinks. As we stood talking with glasses in our hands a number of men who had been chatting amongst us began to talk more loudly across the room to each other and we quickly found ourselves involved in their annoyed questioning about why we workmen were hanging around the streets of Rome waiting for a parade to start when we should be getting on with our jobs. In a few moments, with banging drums, we were led into the auditorium where we found ourselves on the stage playing the part of the crowd in front of the people we had come to the theatre with. Afterwards those of us who had been the crowd were filled with excitement and wanting to tell and re-tell the story we had taken part in. The others who had been the conventional audience had enjoyed the play too, but their conversations were much more about the performance than about the story.

The Gospels are written out of commitment to Jesus Christ and they are intended to generate commitment to Jesus and his message. The message of Jesus as we meet him in the Synoptic Gospels is focused on the core theme of the coming of the kingdom of God. The encounters, miracle stories, teaching, healings, the crucifixion, resurrection and ascension all point in one direction – that in Jesus the 'kingdom of God' is come. John uses different language and expresses the core of the message more explicitly: 'The Word became flesh and dwelt among us . . . full of grace and truth' (John 1:14). The 'kingdom of God' is not defined in the Synoptics – rather its coming is pointed to by story, action, encounter, parable, demonstration. The ruling principles of this kingdom are reality-facing truth, transcendent love and transforming hope that open up new worlds of possibility because the kingdom is where the king is present – and for Jesus that is the world of everyday.

These 'worlds of possibility' are far from generalised abstractions of the sort that litter the history of religiosity like so much up-market waste paper. They are genuine invitations to set out on different ways of seeing and acting, different qualities of belonging in community, because they are embodied – incarnated – in the person, the actions and the speaking of the man who came to be worshipped as the 'Word made flesh'. The invitation is spoken by Jesus, whose own actions open the way for it to be welcomed and accepted. It is the invitation to live practically in hope-filled relationship, rather than to assent to abstract private beliefs kept in a separate category called 'spirituality'. Because the invitation is to live and act in relationship with God through Jesus Christ, responding to it has implications for identity, community, values, actions and opportunities for new directions all of these could realistically take.

These are themes about the 'here and now' of today as much as about the 'there and then' of the Gospels. That is why they stimulate reflection about pastoral practice in the present. They are about practical futures because they are made possible by the call of Jesus for people to live now in the economy (the household) of God. In technical language these themes of the coming of God's kingdom are about eschatology. Traditionally eschatology has been focused on 'the last things' – death and judgement, heaven and hell. In other times all four of these have been recognised as concrete realities. Today, with the exception of death, they have tended to be relegated to a vaguely conceived of spiritualised and distant future – attractive or fearful, but not really much to do with the present.

When I was growing up in north east England one of my favourite folk songs had the lines:

> Dance tev thee daddy, my little laddy,
> dance tev thee daddy, tev thee mammy sing . . .
> thoo shelt hev a fishy, on a little dishy,
> thoo shelt hev a fishy when the boat comes in.

The song gave voice to the hope that things would some day be different from the dreadfulness of the present, but at heart everybody knew that there wouldn't be a day 'when the boat comes in' – at least not for them. Theologians such as Moltmann have argued for the recovery of eschatology as reality-based hope *in the present*, as the motivating factor that gives lively purpose to the believing and actions of Christians. For him eschatology is the vision and energy that brings God's intentions for the future to their beginnings in the here and now.[4] This tension between the 'now and not yet' of the coming of the kingdom means that the people of God are called to live with integrity in this 'time between the times'. That is, Christians are called to live on the doorstep of something that is about to happen and to find ways of holding the door open so that it can start to happen now. The Jesus we meet in the Gospels calls us to a paradoxical (literally 'beside the glory') way of living, inviting people not only to watch the performance, or even to admire it, but get up and take part in it.

For people involved in Christian pastoral practice this can be both attractive and threatening. As I have tried to show, the Gospels as we have them are the foundation texts – holy Scriptures – that arise directly out of the 'pastoral practice' narratives of Jesus and his followers. Any pastoral practice that claims to be Christian must live and tell its stories in dialogue with the stories of Jesus and the stories about Jesus that are in the Gospels. Thus pastoral practice speaks with pastoral practice. Hard questions have to be put from both sides so that the vision, purposes and energy of pastoral practice as part and parcel of Christian mission can be renewed. But for this to happen we need to recognise some of the dynamics of pastoral practice.

Characteristics of Pastoral Practice

The ways pastoral practitioners experience their work have a lot in common with the characteristics of the Gospels I have been highlighting. Pastoral practice tends to have episodes of activity and encounter that appear to arise almost randomly, even if on closer reflection there are many half-hidden connections between the different players and powers in the action. Pastoral practice is experienced as a flow of interlocking and overlapping lived narratives and also as apparently isolated bits of narrative that seem to have no real connection with anything else that is going on. The narratives of pastoral practice, like many of the stories in the Gospels, come to interim rather than final conclusions, and leave lots of loose ends. Indeed, one of the key qualities required of pastoral practitioners is the ability to live with lots of loose ends without giving way to a lust for making contrived connections that will tidy up the story, but which will mask the way to knowing the truth that sets people free. Like the stories in the Gospels and in soaps the different scenarios a pastoral practitioner is involved in at any one time tend to run on parallel tracks then come to crossover junctions that lead the travellers onwards in new directions.

It should be clear too that pastoral practice, however apparently random and disorganised it can be, carries a lot of structural dynamics. This is true whether the practice in question is counselling, a ritual action such as a marriage or a funeral, or involvement in political or social action. Sometimes the structures are explicit as in the stylised roles played by pastor and couple at a wedding, or when required procedures have to be followed to draw down charity funding for a social action project. But, as often, the structures will be more implicit, taking the form of the theoretical frameworks that underlie the ways pastors and counsellors understand what is going on in their communities or clients. A way of dealing with the anxiety that this flow of knowable and unknowable structures generates is for pastoral practitioners to seize hold of psychological and sociological stage theories to help map scenarios such as what can be expected in a child's development, an adult's faith commitments, the development of a marriage, congregational conflicts, bereavement etc.

Stories and structures embody personal and community values, ideals and conflicts. Like the encounters of Jesus with people in the Gospels, and the interactions of characters in TV soaps, the relationships and structures of pastoral practice contain spoken or unspoken ideals and values that are being explored and wrestled with. For example, in most soaps one of the core values is to keep loyalty with your friends and family in all circumstances. Some of the strongest story lines are about people who are caught between conflicting loyalties and who break that sense of solidarity. In the Gospels one of the core values of many of Jesus hearers is to maintain faithfulness to the received teaching of the law of God. This is what it means to be counted as one of the people of God. Some of the strongest story lines (for example the near stoning of the woman taken in adultery [John 8:1–10]) are about what happens when Jesus is seen as subverting or breaking the normal ways of understanding that teaching.

In local churches a core value of the congregation is that the pastor will meet their expectations about how worship is to be led, preaching is to be done and church life is to be managed. The strongest story lines are about what happens when very different expectations come into collision or dialogue with one another. We can see why conflicts experienced in pastoral practice can be so powerful. If loyalty to family and friends; commitment to God's law; the predictability and dependability of community worship, teaching and relationships can all be subverted or broken, what is at stake is not some abstract notion of what we are supposed to believe (as if that is somehow separate from us), but who we are, our *identity*. In relation to stories with values like these, pastoral practitioners are not semi-detached observers as if they were theatre critics, but actors whose presence and practices in the drama contribute to the action of the story and have the potential to show what the story is actually about.

Pastoral practitioners are, then, participant interpreters of stories. Christian pastoral practitioners interpret the stories they take part in, not only from their professional knowledge and expertise, but at the same time out of their experience and commitments as followers of Jesus Christ. As Christian interpreters they will be concerned to do much more than merely re-present the story from a different angle. They will be especially interested in interpreting the story so that it becomes freshly available to their fellow actors in the drama because it starts to be seen in the context of the 'kingdom of God'. The 'world' of the story and the 'world' of God's purposes become opened up to each other. The core values inherent in the stories, together with the structures, relationships and behaviours that embody them, are made available for evaluation, questioning, renewal – as well as for affirmation or rejection. In their roles as participants who have somehow become involved in the personal, communal or political stories they have been invited or appointed to take part in, pastoral practitioners are not simply the bringers of detached professional wisdom from above, but sharers in and growers of the kind of 'inhabited wisdom' that serves to open these stories to the strange economy of God in Jesus Christ.

This does not, however, mean that their role will always be a welcome or a comfortable one. As I suggested earlier, when core values and commitments are challenged by people who threaten to subvert them you get some pretty strong story lines. It is often at the point of challenge that the real core values get brought into the open and the energy available for travelling in new directions moves from being a vaguely imagined possibility to becoming a real life option. Pastoral practitioners who bring these challenges into the open live with the risk that they may just as easily be blamed as complimented for their role. One of the hard questions pastoral practice must ask of the Gospels' witness to Jesus Christ is whether the stories the Gospels bring are likely to prove enabling rather than obstructive in this process.

In some ways the agendas of the Gospels' witness to Jesus are closely related to the agendas of Christian pastoral practice. Both demonstrate the values of the kingdom of God and both call for people to find out what God is doing in the world and join in with it. That is, both are concerned with giving practical and local expression to God's mission in the world. Clearly many pastoral practitioners, even Christian ones, would shy away from any suggestion that their work is directly linked to the practice of God's mission. This is because often the idea of 'mission' is associated in people's minds with notions of having answers before questions are asked; with manipulation of vulnerable people; and with a 'soup and salvation' approach to evangelism. Nevertheless, granted the need for safeguards to avoid these negative associations, unless Christian pastoral practice is theologically linked with the mission of God in the world and with the mission of Christ in the Gospels, it is likely to have no theological foundations at all. Jesus himself makes explicit links between his mission and agendas that are recognisably related to pastoral practice in Luke 4:16–20 and Matthew 25:31–46. However, sustaining this linkage is not simple.

When we take a closer look, the actual concerns of twenty-first century pastoral practice in north-west Europe are often very different from the first century issues addressed by Jesus and his disciples. Here are two groups of examples.

First, some issues faced by today's pastoral practitioners are completely foreign to the world of the New Testament. Many of the ethical questions raised by genetic research were literally not conceived of in Bible times. Although Jesus is held to have a higher regard for women than was common in his day, the agendas of twenty-first century feminisms are light years away from this. Understandings of the roots of mental ill health as arising from combinations of nature and nurture that are commonplace today are completely different from the gospel dynamics with their stories of deliverance from demons. The response of Jesus to disturbed persons was typically to confront the disturbing spirit – very different from the patient professional listening of present-day psychotherapy. Twenty-first century pastoral practice is increasingly concerned with local and global issues of social injustice, fair trade and the oppression caused by unregulated free market economics. Although echoes relevant to these can be found in the Gospels, for example in the 'Song of Mary' (Luke 1:46–48), and Jesus shows a marked preference for marginalised people, eventually himself becoming the victim of religious and political injustice, he offers almost no direct teaching in relation to these matters. Examples could be multiplied, but these serve to highlight the essential strangeness of the world of the Gospels and Jesus to contemporary pastoral practice.

Second, even where there seems to be clear overlap between the Gospel stories and present-day experience, the words for personal relationships and community structures may have described very different realities. Marriage in first-century Israel was a contractual arrangement between families rather than primarily a consensual relationship between couples. Children were the property, as well as the responsibility of parents, well into adult life, rather than the quasi-independent economic units targeted by the present day advertising industry. As children grew to maturity at around the age of 12, they were expected to take their place in the community as adults. The Western experience of protracted teenage years with significant economic resources and without significant responsibilities was almost completely unknown. Families were multi-generational closely-bonded extended communities of obligation, rather than the fragmented and dispersed groups of consent who live in European cities at the start of the twenty-first century. The inner group of 12 who Jesus called were exclusively male and the principal leadership of the New Testament churches was overwhelmingly male, whereas most Western churches in the twenty-first century accept the principle that women as well as men can properly be local and national church leaders.

It is highly likely that people fell in love in first-century Israel and hoped to marry one another; children were loved and cherished by their parents; adolescent offspring did cause their parents to worry about them; families were driven apart by the multiple impacts of economic privation, military occupation and slavery; women did play leading roles in social and religious settings, Jewish as well as Gentile. So there is familiarity as well as strangeness. Part of the genius of the Gospels, as of the Bible generally, lies in the capacity of its stories to evoke a vivid sense of 'being there' such that they resonate clearly with people's experience now. Parents worried sick because they've lost track of their child; a widow following her son's body to the cemetery; people desperate to help sick relatives; a son petulantly leaving home then coming back having lost the lot; a wedding with no wine; peasants, scheming politicians, religious hypocrites – the whole lot are readily recognisable as our contemporaries. Even the crucifixion has become a religiously domesticated scene – until our security in the familiarity of it all is upset by some scandalously explicit treatment that resonates with the violence of today's world and shows it up for the hypocritical, violent and squalid injustice it really was.[5] The familiarity and vividness of the Gospels as they witness to Jesus Christ do serve to reinforce some sense that Jesus is 'one of us' – our friend in the here and now rather than a total stranger forever trapped in the there and then.

This should not, however, blind present-day pastoral practitioners to the insight that where the Bible uses similar words to describe apparently similar sets of relationships, they should be cautious about making over-simple connections between present-day experience and the witness of Scripture. Two sorts of claims in particular need to be treated with real caution. First, the claim that because something appears in the Bible it therefore has God's approval for all time, so 'biblical examples' ought always to be applied to present-day situations. The second is that because a 'biblical model' – for example of family relationships or the way employers should treat employees – has been discerned, its dynamics, if not its detailed content, can be applied uncritically in the present. I am not at all suggesting that biblical examples can never be applied to present-day concerns; or that biblical 'models' cannot contain very important dynamics that resonate with present-day contexts. My point is that just as the Jesus of the Gospels is both familiar and strange to present-day believers, so are the Gospels that witness to him.

If nothing else is clear, this should be. The Bible on its own simply does not work. I mean that although the Bible is free standing – in the sense that it exists as a canon, the content of which was for all practical purposes closed long ago – it has no independent freedom of its own. Although its content cannot be altered, the Bible is not a free agent. The Bible always 'speaks' by joining the people who wrote it with the people who receive it today. It is totally dependent on the relationship between the people who wrote it then and the people who hear and read it now. This is part of the risk God takes in inspiring the Bible writers to reflect on their human relationships, pastoral practice, political contexts, spiritual reflections, etc., by turning them into holy writings that can be available down the generations.

To give oneself in love always involves the risk that what one gives may as easily be misunderstood and exploited as welcomed with open arms, respected, reciprocated. That is what love is like. For God to do this is the biggest risk of all. This is what the teaching and self-giving of Jesus Christ are all about. What Jesus has to say, like all of the words of Scripture, is not spoken into a vacuum, but into contexts and conversations that are ready to be opened up. The Word of God speaking is going to be heard most clearly when the holy and unholy speaking of Scripture is brought into the communities of holy and unholy speaking that pastoral practitioners are involved in. Some readers will be concerned that my speaking of the Bible as unholy as well as holy is showing disrespect for Scripture, but this is far from my intention. What I am arguing here is that the Bible should be taken *as a whole*, including those parts that appear for the moment to be less inspired and inspiring. This is what will help Christians to take the Bible seriously as the reality-facing and reality-renewing witness to the speaking of God that gets heard most clearly in Jesus Christ. The teaching and example of Jesus are confrontational as well as comforting. That is why the hard question must be put as to whether Jesus is more likely to affirm or to challenge the values and agendas of pastoral practice. This is what I will explore in chapter 5.

CHAPTER 5

Do Jesus and Pastoral Practice Belong Together?

The discussion so far has been rather theoretical, so in this chapter I want to highlight six practical areas of concern, each of which leads to one or more questions that pastoral practice needs to address to the gospel witness to Jesus Christ. There is not space to explore these in depth, but a series of brief sketches will expose some of the key issues. These six areas of concern are:

1. The self-fulfilment agenda
2. The demand for a non-judgemental approach
3. The place of forgiveness in pastoral practice
4. Family life as a context for pastoral practice
5. Incarnation as a key doctrine for pastoral practice
6. Curiosity and further revelation

1. Self-Esteem and Self-Fulfilment

The self-esteem of people and groups is one of the most basic concerns of Christian pastoral practitioners. Whether they are pastors, counsellors, community workers or chaplains, they will be concerned to help their clients to have a right estimation of themselves and their worth. This is no different from the concerns of many secular counsellors and community activists, and is not to be confused with the trivia of the self-fulfilment industry. But for Christian pastoral practitioners the quest for right self-esteem raises some key questions. If it is a good and worthwhile self that is encouraged to seek its true fulfilment, what counts as good and worthwhile? What might be the possibilities for and limitations imposed on its fulfilment? These questions are raised in a European context where the major understanding is that persons are discrete individuals with the right to happiness and freedom through the satiation of appetites for economic security, bodily comforts and pleasing relationships, with as little constraint and personal cost as possible. In such a context Christian versions of the self, its possibilities, obligations and calling are bound to be counter-cultural. This is not the place for an extended exploration of the Christian notion of the self,[1] but there are some questions that Christian pastoral practitioners ought not to avoid. These concern the witness of the Gospels to Jesus' sayings and actions about the self, other people and God.

Jesus calls his followers to deny themselves, take up their cross and follow him, since people who make their own fulfilment their first concern will end up losing everything (Matthew 16:24–26). He calls them to humble themselves and become like children if they want to enter the kingdom of heaven (18:1–5). He warns them that that if they assert their own importance they are will be brought down to size (23:12). He reminds them of their calling in the Hebrew Scriptures to love their neighbours as themselves as second only to (a version of?) their calling to love the Lord their God (Mark 12:29–31/Leviticus 19:8). In John 15 he shows that the bonds that join people to one another and to God are the bonds not of power possessed but of love poured out. No greater estimation of the value of people is possible than laying down one's life out of love for one's friends (15:12) – though of course Jesus himself goes a long way further than that. The quality that enables him to do this is his absolute security in his relationship with God the Father. The question that pastoral practice puts to the Gospels can be expressed bluntly. Is the self that the Christian pastoral practitioner is called to seek the fulfilment of, the same self as the one Jesus calls his followers to deny?

Closely related to this are questions arising from the biblical notion that the worth of persons arises from them being created in the image of God and continuing to be the bearers of that image. Is it possible that the 'image of God' in some people becomes so masked by their sinfulness and corruption as to become obliterated, with the implication that they can properly be regarded as not persons at all? This is not just a matter of a detached discussion about whether people like Hitler, Stalin, Saddam Hussein and the like can be saved by God's grace (presumably they could be). Much more importantly, this question is a matter of urgent concern for people who find themselves in danger of being dominated, overpowered, even destroyed by people and structures that show no regard for their humanity and right to freedom. How are people under such pressure to find enough self-respect, motivation and resources to believe that they are worth

something better than this? And where are they to find the will and
the power to relate to their oppressors as human beings who are capable of being changed? It is not out of drawing-room decency, but out
of the demands of the gospel witness to Christ that these hard questions must be put by practical experience to the Bible.

2. The Non-Judgemental Ethic of Pastoral Practice

Pastoral practitioners are in the business of encouraging people to
find their own roads to the freedoms they seek. This means that they
are careful to avoid becoming invaders of the emotional and psychological spaces where their clients are working to find these roads to
re-creation. The liberating combination of unconditional positive
regard, accurate empathy, and critical distance are key qualities of the
pastoral helper. Professional associations who regulate the training
and competencies of counsellors, community workers, and church
ministers promote a profound wariness about the helper engaging in
self-disclosure of their own stories, desires, personal values and religious beliefs. Non-judgemental and value-neutral approaches are at a
premium, especially in counselling and psychotherapy. At stake is the
'professional' credibility of the pastoral helper and the genuine freedom of the people they work with to make the desired change their
own choice. The place of Practical Theology is only maintained as a
subject of study in university departments of religious studies if it
operates in a spirit of detached, analytical enquiry uncluttered by the
prior commitments of religious faith.

There is a whole lot that is right about this. To use one's own faith
to persuade or manipulate vulnerable people into particular ways,
while denying them space to discover and own for themselves the
directions they need to take, is reprehensible. But this does raise the
question for Christian pastoral practitioners of how the ethics of
people-helping that dominate Western secular and church-based
agencies can be related to the Gospels, dominated as these are by
conflicts over the circumstances, faith commitments and vocations of
people facing tough issues in tough places. One way of handling this
tension is to form alternative professional associations for Christian
practitioners, such as the Association of Christian Counsellors, established in Britain as a response to the secularising commitments of the
British Association for Counselling. Another is to offer approaches to
people-helping based in overtly Christian spirituality, such as the
Wholeness Through Christ Network. These are open about the values

and commitments of the counsellors so that clients can, at least in principle, make informed choices about the kind of help they will seek. Making the faith commitments of practitioners and their organisations clear in this way also has the merit of honesty, whereas it could be argued that the claims of value-free approaches are simply nonsense because the claim to be value-free is itself value-laden.

Two core values are commonly at work for secular as well as for Christian counsellors. These are respect for the client as one who is wholly other than oneself; and commitment to sharing the person's journey through receiving their story and offering interpretative comments which can serve as markers on the route towards wholeness. Appeal may be made to the 'model' of *Paraklete* – one called alongside to make strong by their presence – in John 14:26; 16:7f. The most valued approaches in this kind of pastoral practice are those of companionship – being alongside, 'sharing bread for the journey'. Examples from the Gospels that are favoured include the stories of the woman at the well (John 4:7ff); Nicodemus seeking the truth (John 3:1ff) and the journey to Emmaus (Luke 24:13ff). But there are questions that practitioners who claim to base their work in the teaching and example of Jesus have to face. Chief among them arises from the fact that many of Jesus' encounters with people in the Gospels – vulnerable people as well as powerful ones – have major elements of confrontation. The healing and deliverance miracle stories, the accounts of the sayings of Jesus and – most confrontational of all – the suffering and death of Jesus, are all presented as 'tales of the unexpected' rather that stories that go with the grain of what could have been expected anyway.

3. Forgiveness

The theme of forgiveness is central to Jesus' teaching and is closely linked with understandings and misunderstandings about the connection between sin and suffering. A key passage is Mark 2:1–12, the healing of the paralysed man. Jesus tells the man that his sins are forgiven. This leads to complaints from the scribes that only God can forgive sins, so who does Jesus think he is? There is the implied jibe that claiming to forgive sins is a cheap act because you can't see forgiveness. Then Jesus shows that the forgiveness he brings is more than mere words as he tells the man to get up, roll up his mat and go home. The visibility of the healing testifies to the reality of the forgiveness. Here there is an assumed link between the man's paralysis and his sin. By contrast, in John 9 – the story of the healing of the man born blind – a simple connection between sin and suffering is denied and a very ambiguous role is assigned to God into the bargain (John 9:2). Earlier in John, the Baptist points to Jesus as, 'the Lamb of God who takes away the sin of the world' (1:29). Right from the beginning the followers of Jesus have seen the significance of his death on the cross in terms of sacrifice for the forgiveness of sins. In the Gospels then, we see that Jesus recognises the reality of sin and the need for forgiveness – i.e. he embraces the reality that people are cut off by the down-drag of sin from God and therefore from the resources that make for their liberation and reconciliation. In the Gospels the antidote to sinfulness is repentance, forgiveness and reconciliation with the community of God's people. Healings of various sorts are pointers to the reality and availability of forgiveness.

Pastoral practitioners who appeal to the example of Jesus as providing the core values for their actions are therefore faced with hard questions. For among present-day Christians, let alone among secular caring agencies, the notion of sin as the basis for human dis-ease has given way to the notion of sickness; and repentance, forgiveness and reconciliation with the community has given way to insight gained through therapy as the necessary response. This is good so far as it goes. Nobody could seriously want a return to the sin-sodden religion of former times that burdened suffering people with the added weight that they were themselves in some mysterious way responsible for their present condition. But the frequent experience of Christians taking part in counselling training in secular settings, of being assumed to be simplistic, negative and judgemental towards their clients if they raise the question of forgiveness, should alert us to the fact that there are indeed hard questions to be addressed.

The question goes like this. Do Christian pastoral practitioners seeking to qualify or to practice in secular settings have to set aside their convictions about the connections between sin, alienation, suffering on the one hand and forgiveness, reconciliation and healing on the other that they find described in the stories of Jesus? If they do, what are the implications for their integrity as therapists, community workers, pastoral carers, or indeed as persons? Would they be best exercising their pastoral practice only in overtly Christian settings – for example in a church, a single faith school or a 'Christian' medical practice? Or would they be more useful as practitioners who allow their Christian experience and convictions to live in dialogue with their commitments to professional secular codes of practice? And if they take this approach, what resources might they need to help them make the connections that will enable them to retain their integrity as Christian persons engaged in pastoral practice? This is no different from the questions that are faced (or ought to be) by ordinary believers every day as they wonder what it means to be genuinely Christian, genuinely human and genuinely committed to the people they work or live with.

Christians in the West live increasingly within a 'blame culture'. If bad things happen to good people it must be somebody's fault and things can only be resolved if that person accepts the blame. This is a product of the fragmentation of society, where people have poor access to supportive and sustaining communities of nurture, obligation, responsibility and care. Blame cultures foster ideas of responsibility that are simplistic, individualistic, accusatory. Victimisation is easy because it transfers the responsibility from within myself onto something or somebody else, who must be guilty for what has happened to me. In this context, 'sin' is seen as the fault of individuals, and if closure is available at all it takes the form of compensation, but not of forgiveness. Indeed, the idea of forgiveness is scandalous because it undermines the sense that the essence of justice is that those who are to blame must take responsibility and bear their punishment.

In contrast, 'shame cultures' tend to be communities where there is strong cultural identity and social cohesion. If bad things happen to good people the badness threatens not just individuals but the whole group, and the group, aware that something has gone wrong and upset the balance, may look around to identify who has brought shame as a result of their actions. Victimisation is easy here too as the shame of the community is loaded onto those designated as guilty. In the shame culture what counts as 'sin' depends more on the inherited values and patterns of communities of people than on the opinions of individuals. In a blame culture, forgiveness, if it is available at all, is a matter of the comforting of the individual, of the individual accepting his or her self in spite of what they may have done. In a shame culture, forgiveness is mainly about the reconciliation of people to the communities they have offended.[2] Because reconciliation is a community affair, forgiveness is a community affair too. In practice blame cultures and shame cultures in Western society exist side by side and frequently overlap – as for example where traditional Asian communities grow up and seek to retain their distinctive heritage alongside the fragmenting suburban communities of large cities.

In reality the picture is much more complex – not least because the realities of blame and shame have important positive qualities as well as negative aspects. But my point is this. Pastoral practitioners will inevitably find themselves living and working within the complexity of overlapping blame cultures and shame cultures. If they want to appeal to the example of Jesus (who lived and taught in an almost entirely shame culture) as foundational for their values, they will have to put some hard questions to the Gospels as these testify to Jesus' responses to suffering and sinful people. Again, the question is not far away – what resources are needed for these hard questions properly to be engaged with, rather than just vaguely acknowledged or turned into expressions of piety that are fundamentally detached from reality?

4. Family Life

'Family' is another area where Christian pastoral practitioners appeal to the Bible for guidance. Most Christian writing about family appeals to the Epistles for models of relationships within families. But the Gospels are also quarried for the foundation stones that will prevent proper 'Christian' understandings of family being undermined. Paintings of the holy family show them safely at home ('father', mother, Jesus a precious only child, family pets); or the family under threat as they flee from Herod towards Egypt; or the parents confused and awed at the response of the 12-year-old to their desperate seeking. This is safe enough ground for traditional Christians in settled circumstances. The message is that the family experience of Jesus can be relied on to underwrite the values of present-day families experiencing domestic calm, societal pressures and generations growing to (mis)understand each other. This would be fine if the Gospels offered only this kind of picture of Jesus in relation to family, but they do not. The overall picture of Jesus and family is a curious mixture of comfort, challenge and the kind of language that today might be attributed to the leaders of sectarian cults.

The birth narratives set the agenda for Jesus' ministry in extraordinary scenes of heaven and earth coming together. Then there is a silence of thirty years (usually interpreted as the Son of God being content to accept the constraints of ordinary family life), broken only by his disappearance after his Bar Mitzvah. The Gospels show Jesus accepting hospitality in people's homes, even being said to be 'at home' in Capernaum (Mark 2:1), bringing healing to suffering family members, both Jewish and Gentile (Luke 7:1–17), and reinforcing the traditional values of honouring parents that are found in the ten commandments (Matthew 15:4). He calls his disciples 'brothers' and teaches them to make their main title for God in prayer 'Father', just as he did. One of his most powerful parables is a story of family alienation and reconciliation that is designed to call religious leaders to start behaving as if they really were leaders of the authentic family of God (Luke 15:11ff). He uses almost his last breath to ask his mother and his best friend to look after each other (John 19:26–27). So far, so good.

But he also treats his own mother, brothers and sisters harshly when they come and call him to go home with them and stop being so troublesome with his teaching and actions. He keeps them waiting outside while he uses their presence as a teaching point, calling his followers to give higher priority to working for the kingdom of God than to their own families (Luke 8:19f.). According to Luke (14:26) he even says that people who want to be his disciples must hate their father and mother and wife and children. In fact the New Testament is ambiguous about how far Jesus' own family came to share in his ministry and in the mission of the early church. This could be more to do with the wish of the early church to avoid the development of a 'Jesus dynasty' than with any assumptions about their involvement or non-involvement. Obviously the words of Jesus about family, as about everything else, have to be taken in their proper context of his theological inheritance, his first-century context in occupied Palestine, and his eschatological mission, as well as his rabbinic style of teaching with its frequent use of hyperbole and irony alongside more direct teaching methods. After all, he also told people to chop of their own hands if they kept doing wrong things and tear out their own eyes if they kept looking in the wrong direction!

Pastoral practitioners need to be as cautious in trying to find models for Christian standards of family structure and relationship in the teaching of Jesus as in trying to find models for Christian marriage relationships or women's fashion in Ephesians or 1 Peter. The very idea of 'family' carries a whole lot of freight in the form of un-interpreted symbolism and projected fantasies – more so as the shapes of actual families become increasingly varied and fragmented. Roles, relationships and boundaries of families differ hugely across cultures and through time. The idea that one can transpose the idea of 'family' from the Bible into the present, without engaging in careful reflection to try to identify which factors are of universal significance and which are culture and time specific, is simply not tenable. This means that pastoral practitioners working with families have to address some questions to the Gospels' witness to Jesus Christ, as indeed to the

Bible as a whole. These involve engaging with far more of the Gospel text than relates directly to Jesus' sayings or actions about families. To take some simple examples, they could start by asking what insights about family relationships and aspirations might arise out of the Beatitudes (Matthew 5:1–12).

5. Incarnation

When Christian pastoral practitioners reflect on the theological foundations of their work they are more likely to refer to what they do as 'incarnational' ministry than to almost any of the other major doctrines of the faith. When pressed about this they tend to talk about 'being alongside' people and groups in order to 'be with them' in their suffering, their struggles, their hopes, rather as Jesus was with the people as 'Emmanuel' – God with us. This 'being alongside' is often, correctly, rated by pastors as more important than what they might be able to say or do.

This appeal to incarnational ministry is all right as far as it goes. Many people are indeed helped by the quiet, prayerful presence of a godly friend who does not feel the need to make them say or do things that are not real for them. But as an interpretation of incarnational ministry it is inadequate. When John says that 'the word became flesh and lived among us, full of grace and truth' (John 1:14), this is in the context of the creative Word of God; the confrontation brought about by that Word between light and darkness; the reality that when the Word of God came to God's own people they didn't want to know him; and that the coming of the Word in the flesh has opened up the way for people to become 'the children of God'. In the famous phrase of Sam Keen, the incarnation emphasises the 'carnality of grace'.[3]

Far from the incarnation being the clearest sign that Jesus is 'one of us', it is the clearest of signs that God's call is for people to become one with him, and this means that things are going to have to change – a lot. Far from supporting a gentle approach to Christian work and witness, the incarnation as the New Testament witnesses to it is a thoroughly uncomfortable and frequently confrontational idea. It not only shows that earthy humanity is capable of expressing the purposes and the glory of God, but that God's purpose is for people to be renewed so that they can do exactly that. Kenneth Leech puts this in striking terms:

> It is the Incarnation . . . which drives us out to seek and serve Christ in the poor, the ragged, the despised and the broken. It . . .

makes it impossible for Christians to opt for a spirituality which despises the flesh, fears human passion, sexuality and warmth, and shuns the world of politics as squalid and contagious.[4]

Whatever else the Gospels teach about Jesus, they show that he was fully human. Like everybody else he experienced growing up, working for a living, hunger, thirst, tiredness, fear, the need for friendship, the desire to be alone. People recognised him as a man of their own culture and traditions, a preacher, teacher, rabbi, healer who said and did things differently. He had time for people – especially people on the edge – the mentally ill, the demon-possessed, lepers, sex workers, 'tax collectors and sinners'. So Jesus has experienced being a person just as much as anybody else. People knew Jesus' mother and his brothers and sisters; they knew him as the carpenter's son from Nazareth; when he was arrested and crucified he really did suffer; he really did die. These are all realities that the doctrine of the incarnation arises from and points towards.

But there is the other side. When people met Jesus things happened. When he spoke it was as if God had something to say. When he was around people started asking questions about what kinds of lives they were living and how things could be made different. Some were challenged to complete changes of lifestyle. People who had been hopelessly lost or sick for years found themselves free and well and able to work again. So he was a man who made a difference. They used words like 'prophet' and 'teacher about him'. But the Gospels show Jesus as more than that. They describe times when the division between heaven and earth melts away so the very ground becomes the place where God can be heard speaking, where God's light can be seen, where the curse of death is overtaken by the power of God. All of this is brought into focus by Jesus, present to bless, to teach, to challenge, to judge, to call.

But of course, the Gospels were written after the event by people who believed his message. The opening of John shows as clearly as anything can that within the New Testament period itself Jesus' followers believed him to be God incarnate. Jesus was the ground for their faith, the purpose for their life, the focus of their worship, the inspiration for their action, the content of their preaching, the strength for their present, the hope for their future. One of the surprises about the Gospels, notwithstanding the birth narratives, is the general sparseness of reference to angels and heavenly beings – they hardly get a look in even in the resurrection stories. The New

Testament writers were determined to focus on the humanity of Jesus to counteract the teaching of Gnostic sects who emphasised a division between spiritual/heavenly things and fleshly/earthly things. The difference between the Gnostics and the Christians is that the Gnostics believed that salvation could only be achieved through contact with heavenly beings that was initiated and merited by enlightened people, whereas Christians believed that salvation can only be an invitation from God through the man Jesus Christ.

That is why parts of the New Testament positively harp on about the humanity of Jesus. 1 John speaks of 'what was from the beginning, what we have heard, what we have seen with our eyes and touched with our hands, concerning the word of life'. This opens the way for the letter's argument that, 'By this you know the Spirit of God: every spirit that confesses that Jesus Christ has come in the flesh is from God, and every spirit that does not confess Jesus is not from God' (1 John 4:2–3). Even texts like this, however, and the story of the confession of Thomas that Jesus is 'Lord and God' that forms part of the first ending of John's Gospel; the reflections in Hebrews on the sacrifice of Jesus as witness to his divine nature and the testimony of Colossians (1:15, 19) that in Jesus, 'the image of the invisible God . . . the fullness of God was pleased to dwell' do not amount to a full-blown doctrine of the incarnation. Instead the references to the humanity and to the divinity of Jesus Christ that we find in the Gospels and Epistles are expressed as story, prayer, song, testimony, preaching, reflection, worship and even polemic.

The New Testament presents us with practical theological reflection that arises directly out of the worship, mission and actions of the first Christian communities. To put it crudely, as the first generations of Christians told their stories about Jesus, prayed to God out of their memories of him, testified to their faith in him, preached about him, reflected together, and argued with people who opposed them, they came to realise the truth of their own words – that the truth about Jesus was that he was not only a man specially anointed by God (Christ), but God himself. In theological language it was as they spoke and practised the truth that they discovered the dimensions of the truth that is to be found in Jesus and that really sets people free.

This is the opposite of claiming that while the human Jesus, specially endowed with grace from God preached his message in first-century Israel, St Paul and other followers of Jesus 'invented Christianity'. It is when we understand that the whole of the New Testament, indeed the whole Bible, consists of writings that are best characterised as different kinds of practical theology in action, that we begin to see that the encounter with Jesus is about experience, invitation, reflection, discovery, long before it becomes formally the worked out official doctrine that is enshrined in the Creeds that are associated with the Councils of Nicea and Chalcedon.

6. Curiosity and Further Revelation

An important quality needed by Christian pastoral practitioners is a well-honed sense of curiosity that helps them to be open to God's possibilities at the same time that they are professionally aware of the various processes that are involved in a situation. This does not mean being committed to inventing a 'god-script' about everything – or foisting onto people spiritual interpretations that are tangential or irrelevant to the case in hand. But it does mean that pastoral practice that has a justifiable claim to be in some sense Christian must be open to conversations about how the present situation might be understood in the light of the presence of God in Jesus Christ and the witness of the Gospels and the Bible as a whole about him. That is essentially the process that is behind the idea of the base Christian communities that were the energising expression of liberation theology in parts of South America from the late 1960s onwards.

This all sounds fine, but there is a question that has to be faced. If we are to avoid the kind of theological conversation that is no more than people's informed opinions about their present circumstances getting into dialogue with their uninformed opinions about what the Gospels say about Jesus, there will have to be some ground rules about what will count as acceptable interpretation. Otherwise all we get is present experience talking to imagined and projected past experience – very interesting, but not much use. If the encounter between pastoral practitioners and the Jesus of the New Testament Gospels is no more than one set of experiences in dialogue with another set of experiences the Gospels are in danger of becoming mirrors that do little more than reflect the images of their readers, rather than windows thrown open to allow the penetrating light of God's grace to reveal the things of this world as they actually are and as God in Christ is calling them to become. If the Gospels, like Scripture as a whole, are to be received as in some sense the Word of God in the words of men, the Gospels must be assumed to have something worth saying that present experience needs to hear.

At the same time as the Gospels arise from the experiences of the first generations of Jesus' followers, they stand prior to the experience of the people who come to them today for insight, inspiration and guidance. This does not mean, however, that we can find in the Gospels everything we need to discover about what it means to live as Christians in our pastoral practice. Even when the great christological doctrines of the incarnation and the atonement became fully developed and enshrined in the Creeds by the fifth century, the last word about who Jesus is and what he is for had not been spoken. Each generation has to discover for itself who Jesus is for them and what Jesus calls them to be for him.

Although theologians have a major role to play in this process, much of the popular reflection about Christ in each generation comes out of the work of painters, poets, song writers, dramatists, film makers. The work of artists has played a major role in forming and challenging the imaginations of Christians about Jesus: paintings of the holy family and the crucifixion; hymns, oratorios and musicals; poems about journeying with Christ – all stimulate Christians and non-Christians alike to reflect on what living in the present moment with Jesus might mean. The more controversial representations in film such as the *Life of Brian*, *The Last Temptation of Christ* and *The Passion of the Christ* are important because they provoke the questions that if people object to the way Jesus is portrayed here, what was he really like, what was he really about, and what is he really calling people to be and do?

All this provokes another question. Could the compelling encounters that people have with Jesus through portrayals of him in painting, music, drama and film, that 'draw them into the action' also be seen as revelations of the word of God on a par with the revelation of the word of God in the Bible itself? Conservative Christians will reject any such suggestion, arguing that the unique and definitive revelation about God in Jesus Christ is to be found in the Bible and nowhere else. This view has led some Christians to reject any form of artistic portrayal of Jesus as at least dangerous and at worst blasphemous, much as most Muslims reject any possibility of artistic portrayals of God or of the Prophet. But generally Christianity has accepted that portraying Jesus in art, music and drama are acceptable ways of educating people about him and inspiring them in their discipleship. Some contemporary theologians go much further than this. They start from the claim that the Church has always made, that the doctrinal formulations of 'The Great Tradition' are both legitimate and definitive because they arise from a process that started in the Gospels themselves and continued under the guidance of the Holy Spirit (John 14:26; 16:13–14).

David Brown reflects on what he sees as the revelation of God that has emerged in the centuries since the New Testament period. He describes this process as demonstrating 'trajectories of truth'. For most Christians, seeing the Gospels and Scripture generally as linked directly to the Creeds and the life of the Church by means of such 'trajectories of truth' would be acceptable – to reject this idea would amount to saying that the Holy Spirit stopped being active in revealing God's will after the New Testament documents were written. However, Brown pushes the 'trajectories of truth' idea a lot further. He argues: '. . . it is one of the great glories of the incarnation that God chose to identify himself so completely with the human condition that he was willing even to incorporate into himself all the limitations inherent in our mortal nature'.[5] Whatever else this means it means that Jesus was a man of his time at the same time as being God, and that means that *'what God did in effect in the incarnation was commit himself to a developing tradition.'*[6] This developing tradition feeds on 'trajectories of truth' that are in continuity with the revelation of Scripture itself, but that also offer new revelation that stands over against some of the teachings of the Bible as human experience and priorities develop.

Brown applies this idea to changing attitudes among Christians towards valuing women, engaging in social and political action, suffering of innocent people, holiness and virginity, authority in the Church and how truth can be disentangled from fiction.[7] He sees dangers as well as advantages in this dynamic way of reading Scripture, tradition and present-day experience as essentially part of the same living text, for tradition can develop in directions that are bad as well as good. But he insists that if encountering Scripture is to be creative and fruitful for present day discipleship, the idea of the Bible as 'moving text rather than static deposit [is] the best way to characterise the biblical inheritance.'[8] Some Christians will find these ideas threatening because they appear to give developing tradition a higher status in relation to the Bible and the Creeds than it deserves. But for pastoral practitioners whose daily work involves them listening simultaneously and intentionally to the 'moving text' of Scripture and to the 'living human document', the risks inherent in Brown's approach to Scripture and tradition may prove to be worth taking. The results are as likely to lead to conflicts of interest between the claims of Jesus in the Gospels and the claims of present experience, as they are to harmonisations of present experience with the Bible text.

Conflicts of interest provide important learning opportunities. The purpose of reading the Bible in the hope of hearing the word of the Lord is to be open to God's call and follow where he leads. True hearing may come more clearly through conflicts between the text and present experience than through texts that appear to give clear guidance such as Isaiah 30:21. High quality Christian pastoral practice demands sustained commitment to the true hearing of people, communities and Scripture. From this true hearing comes the revelation that things could be different and what the first steps could be. Pastoral practice in the classical definition involves helping people find healing, guidance, sustenance and reconciliation.[9] In other words, among other things, it involves working with people who are hurting, seeking, starving and splitting apart. True hearing of Jesus in the Gospels and the true hearing of people in their hopes and needs could easily give way to direct confrontations where Jesus seems to demand one thing and the present situation the opposite. An example is the contrast between Jesus' designation of second marriage as adultery and people seeking second marriage with the help of the church. Pastors may take either the traditional line that this can never be right because Jesus says so, or they may take a 'trajectories of truth' approach that takes seriously what Jesus says while also giving weight to further insights about married relationships that arise from Christian tradition. Either way, both Scripture and the present situation of the people involved will have to be taken with full seriousness. This two-way opening of Scripture to pastoral practice and pastoral practice to Scripture will help to progress the work of discovering what God's gift of 'salvation' might mean in situations where otherwise there is no reason for any body to expect salvation of any sort.

Christian engagement with the Gospels works from the presupposition that Jesus and his disciples are genuinely our contemporaries. Christian belief, worship and practical action testify to the reality not only that 'God *was* in Christ reconciling the world to himself' (2 Corinthians 5:19), but that God *is* today in Christ doing the same thing. Another presupposition that goes with this is that the Gospels are *localising* texts in the twin senses that they testify to God's actions in Jesus at particular times and places in the past and that they can be expected to do the same in particular times and places now. Pastoral practice must therefore ask how it is possible to engage with the Gospels as they witness to Jesus Christ in ways that recognise them as *both* contemporary and localising text, *and* as having purposes that stretch far beyond the present concerns of a people's limited vision and spiritual appetites. I suggest that there need to be five features of this process.

1. Holy Inheritance

The first concerns how the Gospels are to be received by the people who will read and hear them. All three Abrahamic faiths treat their Scriptures with great respect in their public worship. In churches large Bibles are taken in procession and placed on ornate lecterns that are often shaped like soaring eagles; in synagogues the doors of the tabernacle are opened so that the sacred Torah Scroll can be taken, uncovered and welcomed into the midst of the congregation; in mosques the Holy Qur'an is opened, chanted and read with great solemnity. These actions witness to consciousness of Scripture as holy text that testifies to the word and work of God. There is a creative tension to be worked with here. For Christians the Scriptures are ordinary as well as holy. Recognising this character of Scripture as both holy and ordinary is a vital defence against the tendency to treat Scripture with so much piousness that its messages become fossilised into particular versions of what counts as holiness. For the Gospels holiness is what Jesus demonstrates, speaks and calls people to take part in.

This means that, although the Gospels can be studied intellectually, they will be most truly heard when they are read in the contexts of prayer, community worship and commitment to holy action. Since Christian pastoral practice is Christian holiness in action, engaging with Jesus in the Gospels means facing the hard questions of how present experience and the stories about Jesus fit or don't fit together. When Christian pastoral practice gets into the habit of avoiding this true hearing of the Gospels as holy inheritance it tends to atrophy into church-based social action that is becoming separated from its roots. If the connection between pastoral practice and the Bible is to be maintained the Bible has to be honoured as holy inheritance and pastoral practice has to be characterised as holiness in action.

2. Discovery and Disclosure

The Gospels are holy inheritance, but that does not mean that they should not be treated with scepticism, caution and questioning as well as reverence. As we have seen, who Jesus was and what he was for did not come full-blown to the first disciples when he called them to follow him. In spite of (or because of?) being personally present with Jesus for months and years at a time, the truth came to them gradually as a dawning realisation helped along by moments of vivid disclosure. It was as they thought and talked about their experience of Jesus that they discovered for themselves what he was all about. The Gospels as we have them now are results of that process of discovery. Pastoral practitioners have to follow the same sequence of discovery. This means looking and listening, watching carefully, allowing yourself to be bored, puzzled, annoyed as well as inspired by Jesus. It means developing a nose for what is going on when Jesus challenges or consoles or gives teaching. Pastoral practitioners need to be as argumentatively intuitive about the Gospels as they are about the people they work with. They need to apply their pastoral practice skills and commitments to finding their true hearing of the Gospels. Only in this way will their work be energised by the sparks of discovery and disclosure that are created when the Jesus of the Gospels and our present-day concerns are brought into contact with each other.

3. Reflection

Receiving the Gospels as holy inheritance is about faith attitudes toward the text. Commitment to discovery is about expectation of relationship between the contents of the text and present experience of pastoral practice. Reflection is about discernment of what may lead from encounter with the text to changed or confirmed decisions about what to do next. Pastoral practitioners know that theological reflection, when it is done well, has the blessing of being highly productive and the curse of being very slow. It involves re-running the narratives of pastoral experience and of the Gospel texts, but doing it in slow motion, frame by frame, so that the contributing and conflicting factors can be identified and given their proper weighting. Then the factors and resources that could make the creative difference are identified. Finally there needs to be commitment to action that can realistically be expected to bring about the needed change. This is a far cry from the tendency of practitioners to rush from pressing experience to ransacking the Gospels for some text that they can apply to make things seem 'Christian'. Christian reflection that brings Gospel and present-day narratives together takes time. It cannot normally be done alone and it certainly cannot easily be done alone on paper! It is an activity of people in community and the quality of the reflection depends on the quality of their commitment to being honest with, supportive of and learners from one another. Pastoral practitioners who are committed to engaging with the witness of the Gospels to Jesus Christ have to face the hard questions that the Gospels puts to them about the over-busyness, poverty of resources, individualism and isolation of much of what they do.

4. Disillusion

Disillusion is a key stage in bringing pastoral practice and the Gospel witness to Jesus together. The disciples of Jesus often have the function of asking questions ('Who is this?'), making sick jokes ('there is a lad here with five loaves and two fish, but what are they among so many?') and playing dumb ('O you dull of heart and slow to believe'). They only partly understand what Jesus is doing. Eventually they do make the connection between the actions of Jesus and the presence of God (John 20:28); but for much of the time, as they are taking part in the story, they don't really see what it is all about. For pastoral practitioners the connections between their experiences and the Gospels may sometimes be very clear, but at least as often they may be obscure or completely absent. This is not only because there is a world of difference between the contexts Jesus lived in and those of present-day Durham, Birmingham or New York. The professionalisation of much pastoral practice means that there is an expectation that practitioners should know what is going on and how to bring about the right kinds of change on the basis of agreed values. They are there to use their professional knowledge and skills to change things. Anxiety to perform well can mean that there is a kind of lust to make connections, especially when reports to sponsoring organisations have to be written. In this context the recommendation that disillusion be welcomed as a necessary stage in pastoral interpretation of Scripture can seem foolish and unnecessary. Why not admit candidly that in relation to most present-day situations the Gospels have nothing to say, and get on with the job in hand? Practitioners who are valued most are those who are quietly confident, efficient and inspiring, not the disillusioned.

But the real meaning of disillusion is the taking away of illusion – in this case moving away from a worldview that claims you can always prescribe what is possible, desirable, available. This process is clearly seen in the Gospels. Friends and foes alike have clear inherited ideas about what can be expected of 'the one who is to come'. Most of the problems seem to come from the clash of expectations when Jesus brings completely new interpretations and challenges to what the inheritance of Scripture and being the chosen people of God is supposed to mean. He calls his disciples to become literally disillusioned with all that is expected of the Messiah as they encounter the horror of his crucifixion, and then as they come to terms with their experience of him risen, alive and still calling them to follow. Almost the last story in Luke is about what happens when the risen Jesus, 'was opening up the Scriptures to us' and 'their eyes were opened and they recognised him' (24:31–2). To be disillusioned is to become capable of seeing things as they really are. In this sense disillusion is the threshold of discovery. For Christian pastoral practitioners this means facing the question as to whether allowing themselves to become disillusioned, even with Jesus himself, can bring them to the doorstep of discovering who he really is and what he is really for.

5. Commitment

Every writer and editor of the Gospels had an axe to grind, and every pastoral practitioner works on the basis of their values, loyalties and commitments. The ideas of the Gospels as sacred inheritance, media for discovery, resources for reflection and causes of disillusion are all value-laden. They all presuppose that when people read the Gospels they do so with purpose and commitment. Even scholars engaged in academic textual research about the Gospels need to be clear about the values and commitments that are implicit in their approaches. For Christian pastoral practitioners to engage with the Gospels is to come face to face with Jesus in fellowship with the first generations of his disciples. This face-to-face-ness makes the asking of hard questions in both directions inevitable. Just as the rich man, with his spiritual sensitivity but complicated lifestyle, finds that when he comes face to face with Jesus he must ask 'Good Teacher, what must I do to inherit eternal life?' (Mark 10:17), the pressures of pastoral practice make it inevitable that hard questions will be asked. Jesus' answer shows that he recognises the realities of the man's struggle between the call to holiness and the responsibilities brought by his having many possessions. When pastoral practice asks hard questions of Jesus, Jesus has a way of asking hard questions back. All of these questions are designed to open the way to a reassessment of values and changes or renewal of commitment to godly action. But this in turn raises another hard question which is this: what is supposed to happen when pastoral practitioners disagree about the directions in which their journey with the Jesus they meet in the Gospels will take them? Will the Bible turn out to be a bridge or a boundary between different communities of believers?

CHAPTER 6

Is the Bible a Bridge or a Boundary?

Different Christians, Same Bible

The 'Pentecost vision' of Acts 2 has been fulfilled. There are Christians in virtually every country in the world. The Bible is available in every main language on the planet. Christians live and worship in cultures as varied as those of Inuit hunters in the Canadian Arctic, financial services managers in Frankfurt, wine growers in Lebanon and students in Seoul. Across the spread of history Christians have included first-century Jewish cloth traders, fourth-century Egyptian hermits, thirteenth-century Italian patrons of the arts, twenty-first-century truck drivers from Newcastle. Their spiritual traditions and styles of worship have ranged from a few people meeting to pray in a street-side shack; solitary contemplation; mega-church charismatic celebrations; pontifical high mass; Evensong in an English country church. Among all the variety, two things make for a family likeness among Christians, at least in principle – all find the roots of their faith in Jesus Christ, and all share the Bible as their common inheritance.

In theory the Bible should provide one of the great unifying factors among Christians from the different cultures across the world. Patterns of public worship and church leadership vary widely. Even within a single denomination there can be great variations in styles of worship, roles of leaders and methods of local church governance. Patterns of what counts as Christian ethical behaviour in relation to issues such as marriage, gender roles, ownership of property, etc., show considerable diversity. *But the Bible stays the same.* In spite of the many different translations into different languages, the core text of the Bible has proved to be remarkably stable over time. There has been substantial agreement for centuries past about the limits of the Canon, even granted the acceptance by some Christians of the Apocrypha as part of Scripture. Nobody seriously suggests removing particular books from the Bible or adding other ones to it. Whatever else changes, the Bible stays the same. Any proposed changes to

Christian belief and behaviour have to make their peace with the Bible, not the other way round. In the Bible Christians find the content of the faith story that is theirs to tell and the constant foundation on which the doctrines they believe are built. So the Bible could be expected to be a bridging factor between communities of believers, both in the present and through history. People on different sides of cultural, linguistic, ethical and political boundaries are connected to one another, and share one another's stories, through their common inheritance in the Bible.

Unfortunately, things are not that simple. Christians are divided, not only about how to interpret what the Bible has to say, but even about what position it ought to occupy in the life of their churches. While Christians hear the same words of Scripture, they hear them in different settings. Even in the same settings they may hear them differently. It should be obvious that how you hear the Bible depends a lot on the kind of community of Bible hearers and readers you belong to. Even people in the same Bible-hearing community may savour it differently depending on where they are located in the 'food chain' of their local church; for instance whether they are core members of the leadership or 'fringe' members of the congregation.

Bridge or Boundary?

In this chapter I want to explore two images of Scripture – as boundary and as bridge – to show how local Christian communities' use of the Bible is closely linked to their attitudes of inclusion and exclusion in the way they engage in their mission and pastoral practice. I will begin here with a story about a bridge and a boundary.

On 9 November 1993 the bridge at Mostar in Bosnia-Herzegovina, which had spanned the River Neretva for 427 years, was destroyed by tank fire in the middle of a bloody civil war. On opposite sides of the river were the two different parts of Mostar, one with a mainly Christian population, the other with a mainly Muslim population. The bridge, which was only 29 metres long, was for centuries the only physical link between the two parts of the town. The deliberate destruction of the bridge was a highly symbolic act, for it showed the intention of the men of violence that communities on opposite sides of the river boundary should live for ever in exclusion from each other.

The opening of the reconstructed bridge on 24 July 2004, amid much international attention, was seen as a symbol of reconciliation, and a mark of the intention that the communities should live with their identities intact, but in communication and inclusion with each other. The bridge as a symbol brings into tension the combination of future hope and present reality:

> The bridge has a great future . . . something that is not a mosque or a church, something for all the people in general [but] today the town's Croats and Muslims maintain . . . separation, sending their children to different schools and keeping to their own sides of the river. They even have different mobile phone area codes.[1]

The reconstructed bridge is classified as a World Heritage Site. It was paid for with foreign money. In a real sense its reconstruction was imposed from outside – this boundary between communities must have its bridge. It remains to be seen whether what it is held by international leaders to symbolise will become a reality that is genuinely welcomed and owned by the people who actually live in the separated communities of Mostar.

The Bible as Boundary

When people claim to be 'biblical' or 'Bible-believing' Christians this is often in the context of some kind of disagreement with other Christians who they think are not being 'biblical' in the way they make their side of the case. When people describe themselves as arguing biblically they are making a point about themselves and a point about how they see the Bible. The point that they are making about themselves is that they are in the right because what they believe and what the Bible actually says about (for example) the role of women in the church are the same. The point they are making about the Bible is that what it says about this is absolutely clear and authoritative for all Christians for all time. What the Bible says settles the matter. People who take a different view are being 'unbiblical' and are – by implication – disobedient to the plain teaching of God's Word. Such 'biblical' Christians are treating the Bible as a boundary rather than as a bridge. There are two ways to settle the disagreements when this dynamic is at work. Either the opposition must change its view to come in line with what the Bible says, or they must stay on their own side of the boundary and accept that they will be viewed as spiritually and theologically deficient – living outside of the true will of God; beyond the true community of the people of God.

When biblical Christians claim to take a straightforward biblical stance, say about some aspect of moral behaviour, they are often using the Bible to assert a belief that they fundamentally agree with on other grounds. What these other grounds are is not always clear, even to the people who make the claim. This is because they remain buried underneath the conventional speech forms that are the acceptable ways of handling controversial matters within a congregation. A question that must be asked in relation to this (and it is sometimes hard to find a constructive context in which to ask it), is 'what is it about the behaviours being opposed that is so disturbing to the 'biblical' opponents of it, and how might it become possible for people with different approaches to Scripture to explore *together* what the Bible really says and what it might really mean?' Unfortunately such opportunities for genuinely shared exploration by Christians who take different approaches to Scripture are fairly rare because of the polarised approaches of both 'biblical' and 'liberal' fundamentalists. Meanwhile, ordinary members of the congregation have to make up their own minds about which side of the boundary they will live on. These kinds of boundaries are closely associated with the dynamics of community loyalty.

In 'Bible-based' churches the message of the Bible is clear (or is clearly expounded). Any serious challenge to this line puts the dissident in the position of opposing the Word of the Lord as set forth by the leaders. For example, some churches teach that although women must have a highly-honoured place within the church as wives, mothers or single women, they cannot be allowed to take positions of leadership of congregations, and must only exercise a Christian teaching and pastoral ministry in relation to other women or to children. Biblical texts are cited in support of this restrictive (boundary-keeping) view, such as 1 Corinthians 14:34–35, Ephesians 5:22–24 and 1 Timothy 2:5–8, often without serious regard to their contexts in the Jewish and Gentile leadership and marriage cultures of the first century CE. Women in such congregations have a straightforward choice between conformity and silence if they do not wish to be seen as rebellious, or to leave their church.

Another example is the way the Bible is used by some conservative Christians in relation to formulating pastoral responses to homosexual and lesbian people. Taking their stand on the plain meaning of the biblical texts (and this is indeed clear), often bypassing the question as to why the Bible says what it does, and ignoring the fact that other legal prohibitions of the Old and New Testaments have been set aside by Christians, they act in ways that make the possibilities for serious debate based on *shared* study of Scripture and open-ended discussion with Christians who begin the journey from different places virtually impossible. Gay and lesbian people in such 'biblical' churches have a straightforward choice. They can conform and keep silent about how they experience themselves and the teaching of the Bible or they can leave. The same dynamic applies when people I have caricatured as 'liberal fundamentalists', starting consciously from experience rather than from Scripture, appear to the other side to treat the Bible as little more than advisory or, still worse, irrelevant in relation to the issues.

Theologically and spiritually pathological as these ways of treating the words of the Bible either as either forming a rigid boundary or being an irrelevance can sometimes be, there are other more healthy ways of interpreting the message of the Bible as setting boundaries of various sorts for Christians. These boundaries are set by the existence of the Bible, the messages it contains, and the ways in which it requires responses from its hearers and readers. As we explore these boundaries we will see that when we reach them we receive the call to travel a bit further. To do that we will need to make use of the crossing points or bridges that offer connections with new territory.

The Boundary Set by the Existence of the Bible

The fact that Christians receive the Bible afresh in each generation, in the form of a Canon that is closed, itself sets boundaries. As we saw in chapter 2, a classic definition of the relationship between the Bible and Christian belief asserts that the Bible contains everything[2] necessary for salvation, and draws the line even more tightly by saying, 'so that whatever is not read therein, nor may be proved thereby, is not to be required of any man, that it should be believed . . .' According to this view, people cannot simply make up any set of religious beliefs they want to and call the result Christianity. The definition of what it means to be Christian is that you share in the community of faith that originated in the teaching of the Bible in its witness to Jesus Christ. It might be objected that very few people would be arrogant enough to make up their own religion and call it Christianity, though the rise of a great many para-Christian sects and cults should give pause for thought. But the issue of the existence of the Bible as providing boundaries for what counts as authentic Christian belief and behaviours is much more serious than that, for it arises directly from the kinds of questions that are thrown up by pastoral practice.

Typically, such questions concern what happens when people's quest for release from terrible suffering, or oppressive relationships, or clear injustice, or some form of confusion, come slap up against some piece of Bible teaching that tells them that what they are experiencing is somehow God's will for them. As we have seen the Bible teaches that divorce should only be an option in extreme cases such as the adultery of one of the partners, and that second marriage following that itself amounts to adultery. Does this mean that in Western society, where divorce on other grounds is common and where adults often come to faith in Christ after a whole lot of messy relationships, they should be expected to take the only remaining biblical option of celibacy rather than seeking further marriage in a well-supported Christian context? Or where an illegal immigrant has been employed as a housekeeper on slave level wages and is held under threat of exposure to the law if she protests, is she supposed to follow the biblical injunctions of slaves being obedient to their masters?

The pressures of pastoral practice can act as a kind of internalised primary text within the practitioners themselves, on the basis of which they engage in particular actions without consciously considering first what the Bible or other church teaching might have to offer into the situation. Or they might consider what the Bible has to say, then set it aside as being not relevant to this particular case. This kind of 'gut response' motivation for pastoral practice can be as dangerous and as arbitrary as the rigid imposition of un-interpreted biblical norms. Even where there is some level of careful reflection going on, there can be a tendency to retreat into some kind of core teaching of the Bible. Even if many other things are open to discussion, this at least counts as the unshakable foundation requirements of God. These foundations come in two forms, the specific and the general. What they have in common as boundary principles is that they invite further discussion and exploration at the same time as they invite responses of loyalty and obedience. (Of course, what counts as this 'core biblical teaching' may vary between practitioners, and its selection can be quite arbitrary.) In effect what is being claimed is that the selected parts of the Bible have special authority, while other parts can be safely left on one side. Biblical examples include the Ten Commandments in Exodus 20, Paul's teaching about freedom and forgiveness in Romans 5–8, and the teaching about the unity of God's people in 1 Corinthians 12–14.

The commandments offer the laws of God in a form that anybody can understand. For most believers, most of the time they hold good as godly and practical sense for community living. But what should be the response of pastoral practitioners to people who, driven to despair by the drawn- out suffering of their elderly mother, or desperation by the sustained abuse of a violent spouse, cross the boundary and kill? What should be the response of a pastor when a member of her church, stealing to feed a drug habit, comes clean about his thieving? What should be the response of a pastor when two members of the church, having striven separately for years to hold together their loveless marriages, find comfort in a new relationship with each other? These are all 'boundary' questions that have direct echoes in the teachings of Scripture. There are many others that that were not even thought of when the Bible was being written. In fact most of the questions pastoral practice asks of the Bible are about boundaries between people who are challenged by the beliefs, behaviours and loyalties of others in relation to issues that are not mentioned, or even hinted at in Scripture.

The complex dynamics of pastoral situations with their overlapping stories of need, frustration, sin, failure and searching, produce intense pressure on pastors to give the 'living texts' of the needs of the people they deal with priority over the principles the Bible teaches, however clear these may appear to be. Questions about the boundary issues thrown up by the Bible's call to live in the world in covenant with God and the boundary issues thrown up by pastoral practice are inescapable – unless you choose to abandon pastoral practice or to abandon the Bible. Pastoral practitioners who claim to be engaging in *Christian* action have no choice but to hold them in tension. This can be uncomfortable as well as creative, so it is not surprising that pastors have to find ways of coping that will help them to manage life in these boundary situations.

One of these coping strategies is to base their practice on a combination of broad general theological principles and the deployment of particular, externally-recognised professional skills. So they are likely to propose as 'boundary principles' major claims that have their foundations in the Bible, though without examining too closely the reasons for espousing them. These are expressed as core values[3] such as the commitment to love; respect for human life; respect for personal perspectives on honesty, truth and integrity; respect for property; respect for the natural world on the basis of its character as the creation of God, respect for people's freedom to believe what they want to or need to believe about God. The most frequently-cited Bible text in relation to all this is Genesis 1:27, 'So God created humankind in his own image, in the image of God he created them.' But this more general approach only restates the problem, because establishing such general principles, in the same way as establishing specific boundaries, invites further questions that arise from the tough realities of pastoral practice – particularly, how do you know when the boundaries are reached and what is supposed to happen then?

One way of resolving this issue is to treat the requirements of the Bible as laws that the people of God are required to obey, however inconvenient or uncomfortable that might be. In this sense being a 'biblical Christian' has its own integrity, for at least the rules are clear, they are straightforward to understand and they are the same for everybody. There is a lot that is persuasive about this principle, though successfully applying it depends on two crucial factors that I will come back to in a moment. Seeing the Bible as the Word of God written in the words of men, offering God's laws for how life should be lived, has the great merit of reading Scripture the way Jesus read it. Matthew's Gospel, as we have seen, makes clear that Jesus had huge respect for the law of God in Scripture. Jesus' own religious inheritance was rooted in the *Torah* as well as the prophetic writings. In spite of the many twenty-first-century interpretations of Jesus' attitude to 'the Law' that see him in radical opposition to it, his key complaint about the religious leaders of his time was not that they gave too much attention to the vocation to live the life called for by the *Torah*, but too little.

Jesus' conflict with the religious leaders was over the difference between seeing the law as the embodiment of God's demanding truth, narrowly conceived, and seeing it as the liberating embodiment of God's love, truth, mercy and freedom widely offered. For example, in response to an abstruse theoretical question about the marital status in heaven of a poor woman who had been widowed eight times, Jesus retorts, 'You are wrong, because you know neither the Scriptures nor the power of God' (Matthew 22:29). For Jesus, the truth of God and the mercy of God belong together – they are twin realities of what people are supposed to experience when they are truly open to the presence of God. The Sadducees who asked the question actually knew their 'Bibles' inside out. Jesus response to them carries a double meaning. First, there's a world of difference between knowing the texts and 'knowing the Scriptures'. Second, knowing the texts is no guarantee that a person will also 'know the power of God'. Indeed, the wrong kind of 'knowledge of the text' could lead to the setting of boundaries in pastoral practice that are far from the intention of God.

Neither of the standard core texts of the Ten Commandments and the Sermon on the Mount make any sense at all. They simply don't stand up as community truth. That is, unless they are rooted in the living-out of a practical relationship with the God who gives them vitality and purpose and with Jesus who demonstrates and speaks them. They *belong within the economy of God* and it can be a serious mistake to assume that this is the same as the economy and values of secular Western community discourse.

The 'Sermon on the Mount', for example, is full of the kind of questions pastoral practice is likely to ask of the Bible. In this collection of teachings Jesus deals (among other things) with issues of the relationship between murder and anger; lust, fantasy and adultery; marriage and divorce; truth-speaking and perjury; violent and non-violent resistance; attitudes to neighbours and enemies; almsgiving and prayer; devoted service and divided loyalties, and whether God really can be trusted to deliver on what he says. These are all crossover or boundary questions, not only because they are about the call for the practical service of God through practical respect for other people, but because they deal with the boundary questions of how right perspectives relate to right behaviours and community justice. They are a world away from consumer-driven Western norms of common sense.

Real Contexts and Right Claims

I said at the start of this section that the right application of the kinds of rules of behaviour we find in the Bible depend on two factors. The first of these is that they only make practical sense if they are placed in three contexts and if engaging with them helps people towards making clear decisions.

The first context involves accepting that the Bible does open up the revelation of the word of God. To put it at its simplest, if people are really going to open the Bible to engage with the word of God they have to be attentive to the difference the presence of God might make through what he has to say and the other resources he might have to offer. Without the kind of critically-aware openness that seeks and positively welcomes the presence of God, opening the Bible is no more than engaging with some kind of religious artefact from the past, and is likely to prove more esoteric than helpful.

The second context involves placing the teachings of Scripture as carefully as possible in the settings in which they were originally offered. This involves two things: trying to understand the particular historical situation in which they were first given (where this is possible); and trying to understand the placing and the purpose the teaching serves within the Canon of Scripture as we now have it. As a result of doing this, Christians have come to accept that some of the laws in the 'holiness code', in Leviticus, for example, are no longer binding on Christians, while others are (though where the boundary lies is always open for debate). This process also led the early Christians to conclude that following the death of Jesus on the cross, there was no longer any need for the offering of animal sacrifice in atonement for sin (Hebrews 10:11–25).

The third context is the present-day setting of the Bible hearers and readers. I was once involved in an experimental Scripture exploration group that was studying the Bible's teaching about God in relation to cities and what sort of ministries Christians might consider promoting in relation to the structures and the people of cities. We met for our studies in two different settings. The first was a college seminar room with beautiful gardens outside the windows. The other was an upstairs room in a scruffy church hall on a busy street corner in the centre of town, from which we could see people travelling, trading, arguing, loafing about, being arrested, and so on. Our encounters with the same Bible passages in these different settings produced very different insights into what might count as right pastoral practice. When pastoral practice asks hard questions of the Bible it matters a lot what the pastoral practice is, and when and where it takes place.

The second factor affecting the interpretation and application of Bible rules of behaviour is, to put it in technical language, to what extent the Bible hearers recognise themselves as being part of the covenant community of the people of God and what sort of community that actually is. (This relates closely to the first context in the previous section, but I want to take it further here.) This means accepting that God really is involved and really does have the right to make claims on people's lives and behaviours. There must be two characteristics of this covenant community as it opens up to Scripture in the context of pastoral practice. First, the community must bring to its Bible hearing a genuine diversity of experience. Second, it must be a community of different people that is united in its sense of being called together by God in Jesus Christ. It is an essential principle of practical Christian engagement with Scripture that Bible encounter and interpretation is always primarily a community experience to be shared, rather than primarily a private experience. And it is *always* a cross-cultural exercise.

Single culture and single theological tradition communities are likely to produce increasingly static and conventional hearings and readings of Scripture. It is when the engagements with practical reality that we find in the Bible are separated from this sense of belonging in covenant with God and the people of God *in all their diversity then and in all our diversity now*, that the life gets squeezed out of them. When this happens, the Bible gets used as a weapon in polemical debate rather than becoming genuinely available as living inheritance for the community to own, explore, evaluate and respond to. The difference is between the laws of the Bible interpreted as impenetrable boundaries, and the laws of the Bible interpreted as boundaries that have bridges providing crossing points into the deeper purposes of God for people and communities. It would be a serious mistake to think that this is simply a matter of whether the Bible reader is naturally predisposed as a personality trait to adopt conservative or liberal attitudes to Scripture. Hard questions really do have to be addressed. One of the pressing issues in Western Churches in the first decade of the twenty-first century concerns the question of tolerance and the limits of what can genuinely be regarded as right belief and right behaviour among Christians. I will explore this in the next chapter.

Boundaries Set by the Bible's Messages

Boundaries to the range of diversity that is acceptable as Christian are also set by the *content* of the Bible. The discoveries of archaeology and the analysis of ancient texts can tell us a great deal about the social and political environments, the various cultural trends, and the systems of religious belief and allegiance that were present in biblical times. Such discoveries can also confirm some of the facts and traditions that we find in the Bible itself, though these are open to debate and interpretation. But by setting the limits of the Canon the church expressed its belief that the Bible itself is the unique and primary source of its times for the stories, laws and other writings on which Christians base their convictions about the foundations of their faith in God. The documents selected for inclusion in the New Testament were chosen because they were believed to be the foundation sources of first-hand apostolic witness and first-generation reflections on Jesus himself. Certainly within a few generations or of Jesus' death there was an explosion of writings about who he was, what he said and what it was all supposed to mean. But in terms of the authentic foundation witness to these things by the first generations of Jesus' followers, the Bible is the primary source.

If we had a whole range of such resources – for instance if the Canon of Scripture had never been closed, Christians could be free to pick and choose between the texts that most reflected their preferences. But this is not the case. That is why the interpretation of what the messages of the Bible can be held authoritatively to mean often involves hard struggles over the boundaries of disputed territory. As we will see a little later, Christians tend to resolve this problem by giving the Bible different levels of status in relation to the lives of their different churches. For the moment we need to be honest and admit that the Bible is our only first-generation source for Christian belief and practice, and verification depends on the willingness of Christian communities to allow it the authority that is claimed by its Canonical status. This does not, however, solve all the problems.

In Christianity you can't have a Bible without having an argument. With the boundaries set by the Bible and its messages there are bound to be arguments. This is not because Christians are especially sinful. It is simply necessary. The tradition of argument about what God really wants is embedded in the Bible itself. The argument usually starts with the word 'but'. The Bible has lots of examples of people arguing back in the face of the speaking of God. Moses, Isaiah, Jeremiah, the Virgin Mary and Peter the apostle are all recorded as using 'but' or something like it as their first word back to God. Every time a present-day Bible reader comes across some direction in the Bible that strikes across their experience or their principles, they are likely to respond by protesting that they know somebody that this particular thing might not apply to, because . . .

The point is that the argument with Scripture is not just a protest for the sake of it. The argument always takes place at the boundaries where different territories of imagination, belief, principle and practice meet. The argument is meant to lead somewhere. The protest of Moses led to him guiding the people across boundaries of imagination, faith, fear and hopefulness, as well as of physical journeying. Bible hearing and Bible reading involves not just absorption of the inspiration of past witness, but the call to make decisions about practical living in the present and the kinds of attitudes and actions that will take them from rhetoric into reality. As the lawyer to whom the parable of the Good Samaritan was addressed discovered, when these attitudes and actions involve finding crossing places at the boundaries of what we have thought, believed and practised the results can prove to be both surprising and costly.

The Bible as Bridge or Crossing Place

Often the boundaries in the Bible are marked by water and rivers – the rivers that water Eden in Genesis; the 'Red Sea' in the Exodus story; the Jordan marking the eastern boundary of the 'Promised Land', and so on. Many of the Bible stories that serve as 'hinge points' in the development of the people of God are set beside water and rivers. When a character or the whole people come face to face with a boundary, they often find that this is where old attitudes have to be left behind and new possibilities are opened up. Easy-to-recognise examples include the stories of Jacob wrestling with a stranger by the brook Jabok (Genesis 32:22); Moses stretching out his hand over the 'Red Sea' so that it parts to let the people through (Exodus 14:16ff); Elijah being fed by ravens by a brook (1 Kings 17:2); the exiles weeping by the rivers of Babylon (Psalm 137:1); Jesus being baptised in the Jordan (Matthew 3:13), and Jesus crossing the Kidron at the beginning of the passion story (John 18:1).

The crossing of these 'bridging points' doesn't just connect different pieces of real estate, but different parts of the story, providing starting points for seeing and experiencing things differently. In all of the examples I have just given, a boundary is used as a bridge. I suggest that this must be a key function of the encounters that take place between Scripture and pastoral practice. The hard questions that pastoral practice must ask of Scripture are not rhetorical questions that are calculated to close or cloud the issue and provide yet another reason why something important cannot be done. They are intensely practical ones about how ways forward can be found that could be both honouring to God and means of challenge, blessing or transformation for the people who ask them. This involves taking the opportunities to hear and see familiar things again, but in new ways. We are well used to hating our enemies, but what on earth might happen if we take seriously Jesus' call to love them enough to pray for them, seek reconciliation with them and serve them?

My point is that the Bible doesn't just contain stories about boundaries and crossing over points, but that the Bible, rightly handled by Christian communities, is itself capable of opening the gates to the crossing over points. Authentic reading of Scripture in communities of diversity involves being called to the boundaries of our experiences, preferences and accustomed ways of hearing its voices and languages. It means taking the risk that other Christians may hear the voices of Scripture speaking differently and expecting that God may have more to show us than we were able to see when we just lived with our own kind. The Bible is the common inheritance of Christians, and Christians are called to welcome boundary experiences that highlight differences. Provided that Christians understand that the presence of the Bible invites creative argument, shared encounter with the Bible can be expected to serve as a bridge rather than a boundary between communities of believers.

In the early months after the bridge at Mostar was re-opened, very few people from either side actually used it. They were apprehensive about leaving the security of their own side of the river and crossing over. They were not sure how they would feel and how they would be received when they met as neighbours people they had looked at as strangers who lived on the other side of the ravine. The few who did cross over were able to see their neighbours as people much like themselves who were also trying to make a living, raise their families and rebuild their community. They were able to look back across the river and see their own homes and their own community for the first time from a completely different viewpoint. During the first summer after its opening those who seemed to enjoy the bridge most were young people who met for parties on it and made daredevil jumps from it into the waters beneath. The implications of this parable for creative engagement with Scripture for Christians who have allowed themselves to become divided by the Bible, which should have been allowed to be a bridge, are as obvious as they will be costly to put into practice.

CHAPTER 7

Where in the Church Does the Bible Belong?

A key phrase I used in chapter 6 is, 'the Bible . . . *rightly handled* by Christian communities'. Reading the Bible in communities of diversity that welcome risk rather than automatically resisting it does not declare open season for all manner of religious lunacy. In 2 Timothy 2:15, in the middle of a passage that warns about 'wrangling with words', 'profane chatter' and 'talk [that will] spread like gangrene', Timothy is called to 'rightly explain the word of truth' (NRSV). The AV has 'rightly *dividing* the word of truth'. The sense is that Bible reading that genuinely seeks for the truth requires a sense of discrimination. The Greek word used here – *orthotomounta* – carries the idea of cutting a straight path through the undergrowth so that the way ahead can be found and followed. This takes us to the heart of the politics of Bible reading. Two things are especially important here – where the Bible is *placed* in relation to the local church community, and *the role the church leaders take* in relation to the Bible.

Where the Bible is Placed

I suggest three ways that the Bible can be placed in relation to the local church that affect how it is heard, read and responded to.

1. The Bible Can Be Placed 'Above' the Church

This means that the word of God through the Bible comes to the congregation from 'on high'. In Protestant churches this is often symbolised by a central pulpit placed directly above the communion table (the Word takes priority over the sacraments), and only slightly lower than the pipe organ that symbolises the praises of God. Whether the church is furnished in exactly this way or not, the idea of the Bible being placed above the church carries the sense that 'here is the word of the Lord and there is no arguing with it'. This has the theoretical advantage of allowing the Bible its own voice and the disadvantage that the possibility of surprising conversation with it is severely restricted. In this placing of the Bible, the traditions of Scripture inter-pretation are ignored, or are drawn upon very selectively. The teach-ing of the Bible requires a response of compliance. Of course this does not mean that the people have nothing to say, but if they want to explore or question they will have to do it somewhere else. I once served in a church where the 20 members of the Church Council rarely said anything during meetings, fearing to dissent while the minister was in the chair. One evening after the meeting there was a brawl in the car park involving half a dozen of the members who were arguing furiously about what should have been said during the meeting. I felt, perhaps perversely, that this was a refreshingly healthy reaction to the earlier part of the evening. The pastoral task was to enable the dissent to be brought into the Council meetings where it could make its proper contribution. When the Bible is placed above the church a similar dynamic can apply. Questions, confusion, dissent and anger do not go away. They are displaced and may emerge in ways that are spiritually and humanly very unhealthy.

2. The Bible Can Be Placed Alongside the Church

In church furnishing this model is symbolised by a lectern on one side and a pulpit on the other side of the communion table, symbolising that all of the church's worship takes place within the embrace of the Word of God. In this model, while the Bible has its honoured place in which it is heard and read in the contexts of worship, prayer and study, *both* the Bible and the congregation are allowed their own voices. But this is not a partnership of equals, for in the preaching, teaching and theological reflection that the people take part in, the Bible has its special priority as the Word of God with the people of God. In the *alongside* model the church brings four things into its con-versation with Scripture. These are spiritual openness, tradition, rea-son and an up-to-date knowledge of their own culture and their pressing questions.

Bringing *spiritual openness* to the conversation involves being pre-pared to be interrupted in the routine of one's thinking and actions by what the Bible has to say. This means being open to the sometimes quite offensive challenges that Scripture demands that Christians face up to. Here is a story. Three men were taken hostage by terrorists and two of them were beheaded. The third was held for a couple of weeks and paraded on television looking haggard and terrified with his hooded captors towering over him. The media expressed the outrage and impotence that was felt by everybody. During a quiet mid-week service I was leading as this was taking place I read the words of Luke 6:27, '. . . love your enemies, do good to those who hate you, bless those who curse you, pray for those who abuse you'. I offered a brief reflection on the challenge this put to us at such a time and then led the congregation in prayer for the hostage and his family, and also for his captors. After the service some members of the congregation said that they hadn't realised that Jesus actually meant what he said in that passage and they weren't sure that it was right at all. I encouraged them to stay with their questions and protests and take them into their thinking and their prayers.

Bringing *tradition* into the conversation means considering the ways that other Christians in the past have heard and responded to Scripture. This can inspire reflections that would not be available if today's Christians just brought questions from their present experience and culture. The awareness of being part of the 'communion of saints' of other times and places who have also heard and argued with Scripture makes for a deeper and richer conversation. For example, St Francis of Assisi has become a hugely popular saint with middle-class Christians in the West. Francis read the Gospel descriptions of the poverty of Jesus as a direct example for him to follow personally so he gave up the wealth of his merchant class family and went on the road as a tramp and preacher. Few of the people inspired today by Francis' reading of Jesus teaching about poverty actually want to follow his example. But many are provoked into re-thinking the values their lifestyles enmesh them in and to asking how they can follow Christ with integrity and without pretending.

Bringing *reason* to the conversation means being confident enough to use our minds to ask the kind of questions about the Bible we have been thinking about. This is not just the application of common sense. It is about the Holy Spirit at work in the thinking of women and men today, even as he was in the minds of the people who wrote the words of the Bible. Reason is different from opinion. Opinion may be no more than a view that I happen to hold, however idiosyncratic that might be, and as such it can as easily be the voice of ignorance or prejudice as it can be the voice of experience enriched by wisdom. Reason carries the sense of being prepared to hear other voices, think carefully about what they have to say and be open to the possibility of changing my perspectives as a result. Opinion may be an individual thing. Reason at its best is discovered in communities of reflection.

Bringing *up-to-date knowledge of our own culture and our own questions* involves the people who hear and read Scripture being fully involved with the ordinary things of every day – family life, earning a living, hanging about, buying food, living together or alone, cleaning, entertainment, fashion, politics . . . All of these raise questions about who we are, what we are for, what things we favour and which we want to avoid or oppose, what we think and how we express ourselves. People who are fully involved in the world of ordinary experience and aspiration and committed to listening carefully to its joys and pains are better able to recognise the ordinariness of Scripture in deeper and more fruitful ways than if they keep a defensive distance from it to preserve their faith.

Bringing this openness, awareness of tradition, commitment to using reason, and knowledge of our culture to engagement with the Bible enables real questions about real differences between people to be explored safely and richly. This approach moves Bible hearing and reading away from repeated and increasingly lame rehearsals of well-worn opinions that other members of the church have heard dozens of times before. It is safe, and even salvation-promoting because it places the Bible hearers and readers of today within the community of God's people of other cultures and other times, opening up what Bruggemann calls 'the hopeful imagination'.

Both the *above* and the *alongside* model assume that there is a kind of space between the Bible and the church that hears and reads it. But in the alongside model the space is a hospitable one in which conversation with Scripture – questions, discussion, argument – can not only take place, it is positively encouraged. In the *above the church* model, the rank and file members of the church surrender a lot of their autonomy to Scripture. They allow themselves to have a servant or child relationship toward a parental Bible. In the *alongside* model, the church members are encouraged to hold their autonomy with openness and to have an adult relationship with the Bible that involves respecting the true character of both of them.

An important quality of maturing adults is that they are able not only to live with difference, but to learn from it. This prompts Stephen Fowl to emphasise the importance of 'charitable interpretation' of Scripture. Charitable interpreters will be people who are 'intentional about [becoming] certain types of readers . . . who by virtue of their single-minded attention to God, are well versed in the practices of forgiveness, repentance and reconciliation.'[1] This involves a tough-minded listening to the interpretations of people with whom we differ. It involves, for example being prepared to listen to their interpretations *with enough charity to 'maximise the reasonableness of those with whom one differs'*. As Fowl puts it, '. . . interpretive charity entails both a willingness to listen to differences and a willingness to hear those differences in their fullness'.[2] A good test of attitudes to biblical interpretation is whether they reverence God as God and whether they treat adults as responsible adults.

3. The Bible Can Be Placed within the Church

In the way churches are furnished this can be symbolised by the absence of fixed pulpit or lectern, the worship area functioning as a flexible open space. At first sight the *within* the church model may seem the most inclusive and attractive approach. Put the Bible into the hands of the people, encourage them to read it and talk about what they find there and trust the Holy Spirit to bring out the right interpretations that will issue in holy living. This offers a kind of democratic approach to biblical interpretation and discipleship in the local church. It has the merits of treating Christians like adults in relation to the Bible, and of ensuring that the leadership cannot easily privatise the approved meanings of the text in the interests of their own spiritual and community power scripts. However, there are difficulties that need to be noticed.

First, many congregations, especially evangelical and charismatic ones, place a very high premium on maintaining unity in the fellowship and so seek to minimise difference and conflict, even when there are issues that need to be faced up to. This means that churches tend, without noticing it, to adopt a particular spirituality and social culture that appears to meet the needs of most of their members, but that in reality arise from the pooling of their personal and cultural preferences rather than from the cross-grained calling of God. Even in apparently inclusive churches there can be strong undercurrents of implicit exclusion that can result in the masking of dissent. Open-hearted congregations may not be as genuinely welcoming and permissive, in the best senses of the word, as they think they are.

Second, and related to this, there can be a tendency for the congregation to subconsciously prioritise their own prevailing social and spiritual culture in priority above the Bible, so that they may see the purpose of the Bible as to provide texts that underwrite their existing attitudes and practices.

Third, this approach can arise from an abdication of responsibility in relation to the Bible on the part of church leaders, who are keen to encourage and support the congregation in the discoveries they are making in their encounters with God. The leaders may be eager to play up the 'feel good factor' in Bible study to encourage the people in their use of Scripture. For example they may encourage their home group leaders to major on what we might call the cuddly texts (God is there to bless you) and the power texts (God is there to make you strong and successful) in preference to some of the more challenging texts that may be needed to call the congregation out of its complacency. In this approach the necessary 'distance' between the Bible and the prevailing culture of the congregation is minimised or removed, to such an extent that the prophetic role of Scripture in relation to the church becomes muzzled.

The Role Church Leaders Take in Relation to the Bible

Where the Bible is 'placed' in relation to the church is closely related to the question of how the leaders of the church see their role in developing the relationship between the Bible and the congregation. I suggest two main approaches.

1. Guardians and Gatekeepers

As guardians and gatekeepers, ministers see themselves as having preferential authority in relation to the mediation and interpretation of Scripture for their congregations. Clergy taking this role understand this authority as something conferred on them by their ordination or appointment which has followed a period of careful theological study and selection for ministry. They consider themselves in principle accountable to their denominational leadership for the way they exercise it. This means in principle that the minister is no freer to make up their own interpretation of what the Bible says than any other member of the church. The accountability structures in a denomination mean that in theory ministers as guardians and gatekeepers of the Bible will normally act in some kind of fellowship and solidarity with their colleagues in other similar churches. This approach takes seriously the nature of the Bible as the authoritative word of God by vesting the stewardship of it in people who carry properly accountable authority in the church.

This close association of the authority of clergy with the authority of Scripture puts them in a very powerful role in terms of the relationship between the Bible and the congregation. Probably most clergy are aware of the possibility of abusing this and will regularly use the lectionaries (Bible reading schemes) provided by their denominations. When these are used in association with the liturgical calendar that sets out the pattern of the Christian year with the major festivals and themed seasons such as Advent and Lent, they offer a spread of Bible material to be read in public over 1–3 years. However, even where calendars and lectionaries are used, the minister's role as gatekeeper is further complicated by fragmentary patterns of church attendance. Well into the 1960s in Britain many Christians would attend church every week, so sequential reading of Scripture could be followed through. In the first decade of the twenty-first century, church attendance patterns based on obligation have given way, even among highly committed Christians, to patterns based on religious consumerism, with the result that they tend to be more sporadic.[3] This leads to an increasingly random engagement between ordinary church members and the Bible. An important result of this is that a clear majority of adult church members in the UK, across all denominations, are functionally biblically illiterate. The implications of this for the growth of Christian identity and for the integrity and confidence of Christian witness and pastoral practice in a many-faith society are huge.

2. Guests or Hosts

Hospitality in the form of welcoming strangers as honoured guests is a major theme in the Bible. Hospitality is often present when God comes to speak a strange word, such as in the visit of the travellers to Abraham in Genesis 18:1ff; and in stories of the fulfilment of God's purposes, such as the story of the Great Feast with its overtones of judgement, in Luke 14:15ff. The last teachings of Jesus for his disciples are located in the theologically-rich context of the shared hospitality of the Passover meal (John 13:1ff). One of the resurrection appearance stories in John involves Jesus preparing breakfast for Peter and other disciples before he takes Peter on one side to ask him some questions that are as tough as they are healing (John 21:15ff). One of the hallmarks of the Pentecostal community of the first believers was the combination of welcoming the teaching of the apostles and the joyful sharing of property and of food (Acts 2:42–47). In a major passage about Christian lifestyle and relationships, Paul calls on his hearers to 'stretch out hospitality to strangers' (Romans 12:13). Surprising things can come from practising hospitality. When you welcome strangers you might even find yourself entertaining angels without realising it (Hebrews 13:2). Failure of hospitality is a serious sin that threatens to separate a person from the presence and the blessing of God – indeed Jesus makes a close link between the offering of hospitality and being open to receive the forgiveness of God (Luke 7:44ff). He even links the presence or absence of hospitality to the stranger with the criteria that will be used in the 'last judgement' (Matthew 25:31ff). The prologue of John makes an explicit link between welcoming the Word to his own home and people having 'power to become children of God' (John 1:12).

Hospitality to the stranger can be a powerful symbol for understanding the relationship between the Bible and the church, the Word of God and the people of God. At the end of the day, important though questions are about who owns the Bible and how the Bible relates to the Word of God, they are basically too prosaic, too static to do more than clear the ground for a much more creative and risk-taking engagement with Scripture. In biblical terms hospitality is not about what you share with your family and friends – anybody who fails to provide for relatives and family members is 'worse than an unbeliever' (1 Timothy 5:8). It is about opening the door to strangers who may need food and clothing and rest and a place to stay; and in order to learn from the stories that they have to tell. Hospitality does not involve taking away the core identity of the stranger *as stranger*, and making them 'one of us'. It is much richer than that, for it involves allowing the stranger to retain their difference at the same time as recognising that you and they belong together, at least for a time, in the same place. As a result of that belonging new things, previously unimagined, become genuine possibilities. Samaritans and Jews might even discover that they belong together (Luke 10:30ff).

In the Bible, hospitality is closely linked to the idea of visitation. The stranger comes from a distance, stays around for a while for a purpose, then continues on their journey.[4] The one who is received with hospitality, however generously, retains their otherness, their own integrity; and this means that the host also retains their identity, their integrity. The guest may certainly make their presence felt, but after they have continued on their way, the host is left to reflect on what has changed that would not have changed otherwise as a result of the encounter, and to reflect on what will stay different as a result of what has been said, shared, argued about, explored. In this sense, the action of offering hospitality to the stranger is at the same time the action of opening up oneself and one's community to the possibility of coming under scrutiny or judgement that exposes the need for changes of perspective, attitude and activity. For in a biblical understanding, visitation is closely linked to the idea of judgement and of new things beginning in response to God's call. Three examples of this in the Gospels are provided by Jesus as a guest of a Pharisee (Luke 7:36ff); the call of Zacchaeus (Luke 19:1ff), and Jesus' resurrection appearance to his disciples (John 20:19ff).

Openness and curiosity are important aspects of hospitality. Openness is about having emotional, psychological and spiritual space within oneself so that there is room for the stranger to come near, rest and be refreshed, and offer the gifts of wisdom, encouragement and challenge that they bring. 'Open-hearted' and 'open-handed' are phrases that capture this well. People who have an over-strong need to defend their physical, emotional and spiritual space (their boundaries) find the openness required by the call for hospitality difficult to sustain.

The curiosity that goes with this openness involves being ready to learn from the stranger. This is a non-intrusive curiosity, that offers its questions in open ways that leaves the guest with freedom to respond in their own way. It is the kind of curiosity that is open to learn, but that does not lead to interrogation as a step towards the kind of possessiveness that seeks to change the stranger from one's guest (or host) into a mirror image of one's self. This curiosity towards the Bible is hard for Christians because they experience the Bible as 'the old, old story' that they are (or should be) familiar with. Like the Creeds, the Bible holds no surprises. They *know* what it says and what it means. Without this basic openness and curiosity towards the Bible, it will not matter what hard questions pastoral practice asks of Scripture because the answers will be ready to be spoken before the questions are even asked. The whole point of having Scripture as the Word of God who speaks and who keeps on speaking will be completely missed.

Seeing the relationship between the Scripture and the Church in terms of hospitality where the church is sometimes the host, sometimes the guest, is a very fruitful and profoundly biblical notion. It cuts through the models of above, alongside, within by putting human hierarchies in their place and rejecting the expectation that the agenda of the Bible and the agenda of twenty-first century Christians are always, or mostly, likely to be the same. It is comparatively easy to reflect on how useful the image of the Bible as guest or host might be when it applies just to the relationship between the Bible and a particular local church, in which people are mostly agreed about their forms of worship, the cultures of their fellowship and their expectations of what counts as Christian moral behaviour.

But what might happen if people from *different* churches or *different* Christian cultures were to come together as guests of the Bible, or to be together *with their differences*, offering the Bible the hospitality of holy listening and shared practical reflection? What might happen if Christians were to read the Bible with non-Christians on this basis? There is no reason why, within the generous and safe context of hospitality, people with strong differences should not express their differences strongly and with courtesy. The constraints of hospitality should in principle preclude the compulsion to require one's fellow guests to agree. The conversation might sometimes have to be left incomplete, leaving the different guests to reflect further after the encounter; but always the experience of offering and receiving this depth of hospitality leaves open the possibility of further meeting, further exploration, even of changes in perspectives and actions.

As I have tried to show, the biblical notion of hospitality is closely bound up with the challenging and transforming presence of the stranger. Being jointly guests at the same table with Scripture as the host, or being the host where Scripture and other strangers are one's honoured guests should at least limit the possibilities of the Bible being used as a manipulative tool or an offensive weapon in one's own cause. This is far more than a call for Christians to be reasonably civilised in the way they relate to one another. God's call is not a patronising pat on the head for siblings who don't really get on, with the injunction that they should play nicely together like good children of their heavenly Father. The fact is that genuinely Christian engagement with the Bible involves getting to grips with differences that are passionately held. Because Christian pastoral practice is so closely related to Christian mission it must be a passionate business both in technical theological terms (it involves close and committed engagement with people who suffer and who need 'salvation'); and in terms of the energy charge that is often around as people struggle with the boundaries of their capabilities, beliefs, knowledge, resources, etc. There are bound to be disagreements, so it would be useful if the Bible could be appealed to as having the authority of God's final Word on all subjects over which Christians might differ. Surely if Christians could agree to this, then the room for conflict over boundaries of belief and behaviour would be greatly reduced.

But, as I have already shown, you simply cannot have a Bible without having disagreements and questions among its hearers and read-ers. One of the questions pastoral practice asks of the Bible concerns what needs to happen when Christians disagree about what Scripture actually says or about the weight that what it says should carry. One way to explore this is to take a core value about religious practice that is common to Western society in general and to the churches, and reflect on some of the ways it might speak to the agenda of pastoral practice. The core value that I have chosen for this is 'religious tolera-tion'. This is, of course a huge topic that really requires a whole book to itself, so the discussion that follows will necessarily be a sketched outline.[5]

Religious Toleration

Toleration is one of the hallmarks of a civilised and progressive soci-ety. In the cosmopolitan societies of the twenty-first century, espe-cially after the religious and racial conflicts that have been exacerbated since 9/11, the practice of religious toleration is essential to the maintenance of international peace and civil order, as well as to promoting the contribution to public life of distinctive religious and ethnic groups.[6] It should be obvious that twenty-first century Christians have a vested interest in promoting the values of religious toleration. After all, they want freedom to worship, to teach and to witness to their faith just as much as members of other world faiths.

So what are the possibilities of bringing together this public value and some of the questions pastoral practice asks of the Bible? At first sight the prospects do not look at all promising, for we have a Bible that is full of examples of religious intolerance, especially – but not exclusively – in the Old Testament. And today's Christians are inher-itors of the traditions of a Church that, when its fortunes have become closely linked with those of dominant political power structures, has not hesitated to visit violent persecution on its own dissidents and minorities. Christian intolerance towards fellow Christians, toward those of other world faiths, and towards powerless members of soci-ety has helped to fuel the realities of social exclusion, ethnic division and political injustice. The actual subject matter of the theological and political argument agendas have varied over time. Obvious front line examples for twenty-first century Western churches include what counts as acceptable shapes of family and marriage relationships; the role of women in church leadership and wider society; the power dynamics between the communities and churches of the Global South and the Global North; same gender sexual relationships; the legitimacy of violence as a means of defending the rights of ethnic faith communities; the limits of diversity of belief that can be held to be compatible with the unity of the body of Christ, and the legitimacy of evangelism directed toward people of other faiths.

These are not issues about which Christians hold a variety of personal opinions which they are happy to discuss and, where necessary 'agree to disagree'. They are increasingly seen as essentially 'creedal' or 'church-dividing' issues. At the heart of the conflicts are arguments about what kind of Christian belief and practice can properly be regarded as faithful to the witness of Scripture and authentically Christian tradition. In the context of our exploration the hard question pastoral practice asks is, 'how far can the Bible be seen as a bridge between communities of Christian believers who come with real passion at the same questions from different sides of the boundaries?' Or, like the repaired Bridge of Mostar, does it just stand there as a symbol of the hope that perpetually disappoints because too few people are prepared to use it to really meet each other.

At this point we might think that the project of using the Bible to help us with the question of religious toleration is likely to be so difficult or so costly that it will be a waste of time. But this is precisely where the Bible, read in communities of hospitable difference, *can* help. This is because from beginning to end, the subject matter of the Bible is concerned with how people relate to boundaries and bridges of covenant, circumstance, community, belief, practical discipleship, imagination, mission, and facing and overcoming the 'principalities and powers' of ungodliness and evil. As boundary differences are allowed their reality in the context of God's call to go beyond the normal limits of human hospitality and vision, they become places where renewal of faith passes into the practical actions that embody the mission of God.

Backwards and Forwards

But for this to become reality, not just rhetoric, it is important to get hold of an important pastoral principle of engagement with Scripture. The Bible is about *faith written backwards in order that God's people can be called to move forwards.* Every word of the Bible was written by people who were reflecting on the experiences that are described there; had inherited the stories and faith traditions they were enjoying or pushing against; had themselves or through others experienced the calling, hope, alienation, joy or despair of which they wrote. In practical theology terms the historical narratives and apocalyptic visions, as much as prophecy, prayers and letters, are written out of theological reflection on experience. The purpose of this *reflection backwards* is to provide the vision and momentum to enable God's people to open their eyes and their minds rather than closing ranks when they come to boundaries that challenge their experience and assumptions about God's purposes. As a result of giving these challenges house room (hospitality) some of the inheritance of the faith tradition will be confirmed, some will be renewed and some will be opened up for re-interpretation.

The *'Bible as faith written backwards'* principle means that the Bible will first be received as stories and testimonies of communities whose faith we share, not as free-standing collections of sayings or doctrinal or ethical prescriptions. This does not mean that Scripture ceases to be authoritative for Christian belief and action, for it is the foundation witness to the faith, centred on the person, the actions and the call of Jesus Christ. But it does mean that when pastoral practice puts questions to the Bible, it has at the same time to provide enough hospitable space for the questions to be properly explored – space in which the Bible can be allowed its own integrity and its own voices that can engage in conversation that actually leads somewhere. This is very different from recycling past formulas or acceptable pieties in a home group that has gone solid. This kind of Bible reading has a robust relationship with the realities of pastoral action.

Religious toleration is about what it means to maintain proper (Christian) confidence and identity at the same time as facing up to questions about the limits of diversity of belief, belonging and action. Far from being an intellectual exercise about airy theological principles, it is a matter of life and death in which the survival of individuals and of whole faith communities against the onslaughts of religious and political bigotry is at stake. Where is the boundary to be drawn between those who are in the covenant community because they are faithful to the truth and righteousness of God, and those who choose to remain on the other side of that boundary?

Many parts of the Bible address this question directly – in the Old Testament Daniel is an obvious example as he and his companions are pressurised to compromise their principles about diet, worship, and the legitimacy before God of pagan political power. The limits of theological diversity as the priority of God's call, and the tension of this with realities of life in the company of God's people, is the background and the foreground of Deuteronomy and of Leviticus. Throughout the Old Testament the question is how to live faithfully as God's people Israel, what happens when you don't and what happens after that. The issue of God's purposes for the rest of the nations arises from time to time, but is addressed either by declarations that the 'nations' are under the judgement of God, or are to find in the example of Israel the light that will call them out of darkness. There are some tantalising exceptions to this in the forms of individuals who come from outside the community of Israel to speak or act in God's name towards God's people, and who stand as signs that God has purposes for people that reach beyond the boundaries of faith and imagination of his 'chosen' people. 'This means that being children of the covenant does not mean that you are the only people loved by God. It rather means that God has a special vocation for you that it is your obligation to fulfil.'[7] In the story of Jonah, the prophet is thrown into confusion and despair as the people of Nineveh actually repent in response to his preaching. If the limits of diversity are so clear to the prophet, why do they seem to unclear to God?

The question of the limits of diversity becomes more pronounced in the New Testament as Jesus himself both affirms the importance of the *Torah* and overturns a whole range of popular Jewish beliefs that were based on it, including interpretations of Sabbath observance, purity laws, who you could eat with, who really counts as your neighbour, who has the right to pass judgement on whom, and so on. For the earliest church the 'limits of diversity' question was focused, as we have seen, on the question of whether Gentile converts should have to become Jews in order to be proper Christians. It is clear from the New Testament that although this issue began to be resolved early on, as we see in Acts 10–15, it was a problem that rumbled on for decades, probably until well after the fall of Jerusalem.

If questions of right belief and the right to belong were difficult enough for the early church, questions about the limits of diversity of moral behaviour are common throughout the Bible and are just as difficult to handle. Questions about faithfulness in marriage, the legitimacy of divorce, whether to eat meat that had been used in pagan temple sacrifices, how slaves should relate to slave owners, parents to children, what action a property owner should take against a thieving slave, and how Christian citizens should respond to pagan rulers are just a few examples. Lists of outrageous sins give an indication of some of the limits of expected behaviour (1 Corinthians 6:9–11). Other lists of virtues and fruits of the Holy Spirit show clear evidence that when people became Christians they were expected to experience radical changes of behaviour and lifestyle as evidence of their spiritual transformation.

The notion of religious toleration can seem a rather lofty one for ordinary Christians to have to take seriously. But the examples of what is commanded, allowed or forbidden in the Bible are not only surprisingly earthy, but are also open for discussion and even dissent by believers today. It is clear that the mere fact that something is forbidden in Scripture (for example, women speaking in church, wearing elaborate hairstyles and being fashion conscious) is no guarantee that modern-day Christians will treat this as binding. This is even more clear in relation to the food laws in Leviticus, the teaching of parts of the New Testament about divorce, the commitment to circumcising men who belong to the people of God and how to make clothes, to name just a few examples. It is often said that different parts of the Bible contradict each other, and this is true. So there must be a commitment to finding principles about which parts of Scripture must be regarded as binding for all time and which can be regarded as useful for teaching about the background of God's people, but need not be seen as binding on all God's people today.

Keith Ward commends six principles that need to be applied to find out 'what the Bible really says'.[8] One of these he calls 'sublation'. This is the approach of taking the literal meaning of a passage and finding another passage in the Bible that serves to bring out its deeper spiritual meaning, while leaving the original literal meaning behind. Jesus himself does this in his repeated use of the formula, 'You have heard it said . . . but I say to you' (Matthew 5:21, 27, 31, 33, 38, 43). Within this set he takes a saying directly from the Law – 'an eye for eye and a tooth for a tooth' but tells his hearers ' Do not resist an evil person . . .' (Matthew 5:38f). Another example Ward gives is the way Jesus reinterprets Psalm 139:21f, 'Do I not hate them that hate you, O Lord . . .', telling his disciples, 'Love your enemies . . .' (Matthew 5:43).[9]

Faithful people will have different opinions about which texts can be seen as 'sublated' by which other texts. 'What, then does the Bible do? It upsets our pre-conceived ideas, puts in question our over-neat systems of doctrine, presents paradoxes and conflicting viewpoints . . . But above all, it turns the mind to God in reverence and praise rather than comprehension and explanation.'[10] The fact that there is variation within Scripture about how the call of God is to be discerned should alert Christians to the need to resist single-voiced interpretations, especially when the result will lead to discrimination being practised against people who are too poor or too powerless in relation to their circumstances to live differently, even if it is right for them to do so. One of the most important energising factors in religious intolerance displayed by Christians is single-voiced and privatised readings of Scripture by people who know what the Bible *really* means and *that it can mean only that.*

This does not mean that Christians can never discriminate between true and false readings of Scripture as if all possible readings, however contradictory, are equally valid. That would mean that everybody could be free to be their own isolated Bible interpreter and there would be no point in having a Bible at all. There are examples in the Bible of Christians coming to the point of breaking fellowship with people they have come into conflict with. Most of these concern cases of pastoral discipline where, every effort having been made to call the offenders back to holy living, the church is called to send them out, with the intent that they will then repent and return (Matthew 18:15–17; 1 Corinthians 5:1–7; 2 Corinthians 2:5–11). Other examples of pastoral discipline concern what is to be done when the well-being of a local church is threatened by false teaching or by immorality among the leadership, such as we find in 2 Timothy 4:3, Revelation 2:15 and Revelation 2:20ff. The issue of what counts as the acceptable limits of Christian belief and the criteria that define the authentic witness to Jesus Christ lies behind the whole discussion in 1 John – see especially 4:1–7. Most significantly for our discussion, the whole context of the argument in 1 John about what counts as true and false teaching is focused on the centrality of belief in Jesus who came in the flesh and his call to love one another as God has loved us. The call to hospitable love in relating to people who disagree is one of the hallmarks of the New Testament: that differences – even major ones such as the Jewish–Gentile controversy, which was a church-dividing issue if ever there was one – should be addressed by communities of difference who are actively and strenuously seeking reconciliation with God and with one another. This means that they will not have prejudged the issues before they have worked together on the questions that threaten to divide them. Lest all this sound a bit like the measured and polite disagreement of an academic discussion, it is important to bear in mind the blazing passions and blunt language that were generated as some of these differences were being faced up to – see Galatians 2: 11ff; Revelation 3:9.

Toleration Is Not Enough

Establishing religious toleration in a society is a great step forward, but in itself it is not enough. The New Testament witness to the mission of the gospel being carried forward by communities of difference who are seeking reconciliation with one another and with God should alert us to the fact that religious toleration is simply too low a level of relationship for Christians to aim for. I have a poster in my office of a street preacher carrying a placard that reads, 'Tolerate thy neighbour'. Underneath the caption reads, 'I'm a pragmatist!' By itself, the notion of religious toleration can be a grim idea. It means accepting that differences will always be there and agreeing not to fight over them. This at least is progress when you consider the fantastically high levels of violence visited by 'Christians' against each other until recent times. But in itself accepting the realities of difference while refusing to explore them is like having a new bridge but refusing ever to cross it. The writers of the New Testament witness to a reality that is much higher, much more creative than a sad and sullen truce with people who are supposed to be our brothers and sisters. As Paul makes clear, Christians are called to witness to the practical reality of what they believe by the quality of how they live together and by the content of their message. One without the other is unconvincing. They are to be communities of tough-minded reconciliation who live and teach as 'ambassadors for Christ' (2 Corinthians 5:16–22). A disconcerting way to discover some of the boundaries they had to negotiate among themselves to be this kind of community is to read Colossians 3:1–11 and reverse every phrase.

It takes a lot of grace, a lot of courage and a lot of commitment to seek reconciliation by crossing a bridge when the people you have come to believe in as your enemies are waiting to meet you on the other side. It seems clear to me that the Bible will only become available as a bridge rather than as a boundary between communities of believers if they seek the grace and strength to take the first steps on that journey. All that makes people human because they are made 'in the image of God' is likely to be challenged by this kind of journey, but it is among the sounds of communities of difference that the Bible will be heard to speak most clearly. Faced with such challenge to our humanity we will be forced to face another hard question pastoral practice asks of the Bible. Is it possible to be both human and biblical at the same time?

CHAPTER 8

Can We Be Human and Biblical at the Same Time?

At first sight this question hardly seems worth exploring. The people using the Bible pictured in chapter 1 were all trying to be human and biblical at the same time, so what's the problem? People use the Bible, so they *are* being human and biblical. Against that response, I suggest that this is one of the toughest of the questions that pastoral practice asks of the Bible. Asking whether we can be human and biblical at the same time involves exploring whether being biblical imposes restraints on what it means to be human – effectively taking away human freedom – or whether being biblical as Christians is likely to release greater possibilities for freedom and human creativity. Put more simply, is being biblical likely to make people narrower as persons or bigger as persons? Does submitting to the purposes of God as they are revealed in the Bible serve to diminish what Paul calls the 'freedom of the glory of the children of God'; or does it work to release this through renewal of the perspectives, relationships and actions that make up Christian practice?

It is worth pausing to recognise that all the other questions that have formed the chapter headings in this book are themselves ways of asking whether we can be human and biblical at the same time. Now we need to put the question more explicitly. Each of the other questions could be answered in terms of intellectual theories about the Bible and its history, though I have tried to avoid this by earthing the enquiry in practical illustrations. Within each section I have assumed that for Christian pastoral practitioners the Bible must be far more than merely foundational for values, beliefs and actions. Foundations are vital, but you can't eat, sleep, play games or socialise in them for very long without getting bored and uncomfortable. You want to actually live in the household, go out built up by its resources, come back with questions, stories, new ideas, work together on these in the confidence that you can know who you are and where you belong. Because of this inward and outward movement of living in the household, people are free to grow and change. They can go out of the comfort zone of the household with enough confidence to engage with the tensions that are thrown up by God's persistent lack of interest in much of conventional religion combined with his habit of interfering in the world of everyday things.

Jesus captures this idea in the picture of the sheepfold in John 10. The sheep know where they belong because they know who they belong to. They feel safe because they recognise the voice of the one who provides for and protects them. Entering through the gate provided by the shepherd they 'will be saved, and will come in and go out and find pasture' (John 10:9). This rhythm, based in secure belonging, of coming in and going out to find pasture *which is outside of the fold* opens the way for 'having life, and having it in all its fullness'. Jesus presses the illustration much further, however, than stopping at the point where his 'sheep' have fullness of life. He goes on to speak of deadly threat, conflicting voices, the willing laying down of life both for these sheep and 'other sheep that are not of this fold'. Here Jesus was using a parable that was already a 'scriptural illustration' long before he was born.[1] He was using it in a way that was faithful to the harshly worded messages of the original. This broke through the familiar assumption that the role of the 'good shepherd' was limited to the nurture of 'us and our kind' and emphasised the danger and sacrifice that must be involved. For Jesus the work of the pastor (which literally means shepherd) involves the purposeful crossing of boundaries for the sake of others, even at the risk of life itself. In this way, we may reflect, Jesus was demonstrating what it could mean for him and his followers to be human and biblical at the same time.

The question of whether we can be human and biblical at the same time contains three important words that look simple enough, but are actually quite slippery if we open them up to theological reflection. If we do not open them up in this way we risk them being hijacked and used in the name of Christianity in ways that may be described without exaggeration as promoting religious exclusion or even religious terrorism. The words are 'we', 'human', and 'biblical'. These offer three further questions: who are 'we'?, 'who is human'?, and 'what is 'biblical'? I will take them in reverse order.

What is 'Biblical'?
1. Present in the Bible

As we saw earlier, when people claim that some value or action they are promoting is 'biblical' they mean that it appears in the Bible and this is their main ground for authority in staking their claim. It is biblical in this sense to require that people live to worship the one true God; determinedly resist substituting man-made images for God; refrain from using the name of God as a swear word; observe the Sabbath principle; honour their parents; refuse to commit murder, adultery, and perjury; and avoid lusting after their neighbour's wife, female slave, ox or donkey (Exodus 20:1–17). It is biblical in the sense of being present in the Bible to 'do justice, and to love mercy, and to walk humbly with your God' (Micah 6:8). It is biblical in this sense to love your enemies as well as your neighbours (Matthew 5:38ff) and to resist evil with responses of goodness (Romans 12:17).

But it is also biblical in the sense of being present in the Bible to expect that women should be silent during public worship (1 Corinthians 14:34); to drive a spike through the ear of a volunteer slave (Deuteronomy 15:17); to commit mass execution of one's religious opponents (1 Kings 18:40), and to drink poison and handle deadly snakes without ill effects and with possible benefits to others (Mark 16:18). Obviously, the mere presence of something in the Bible, *even when it is apparently commended in the name of God*, cannot in itself be taken as a good enough foundation for present-day Christian practice.

Even when something is commended in the Bible for practice by the followers of Jesus – such as the 'Lord's Prayer' in Luke 11:1–4, or the approach to evangelism he gives in Luke 10:1–12, it does not require a response of simple endless repetition of a past formula until the return of the Lord. It does require imaginative engagement with the spirituality, culture and practices of the text so that present-day prayer and action can be well founded in the Word of God, be in radical continuity with the faith Jesus taught, and be genuinely open to the tough-minded and gracious purposes of God in the present.

One of the funny stories in the Gospels illustrates this point (po-faced liturgical readings of Scripture often hide the mischievous tone of voice in some of the stories and miss the entire point). In Matthew 18:21 Peter asks Jesus, 'If my brother sins against me, how often should I forgive him? As many as seven times?' Jesus replies, 'Not seven times, but seventy times seven.' Peter's imagination about mercy and forgiveness has already been stretched to the limit in being able to conceive of forgiving a brother as many as seven times (a holy number). Jesus blows this puny idea apart with his apparently tongue-in-cheek talk of seventy times seven. Obviously Jesus isn't saying that you can put up with your brother 449 times then give him hell after the 450th time. Such stretched-out calculation of the scores has no part in forgiveness. The joke is used to emphasise the life-saving power of mercy and the deadly seriousness of forgiveness, as the parable of the unjust steward which follows this passage shows. In fact, when Jesus replies to Peter's question he is using a quotation from Genesis, but reversing its meaning: 'If Cain is avenged sevenfold, truly Lamech seventy-sevenfold' (Genesis 4:24). As he pushes home the message about the unlimited mercy of God, Jesus is being human and biblical at the same time both by taking Scripture seriously and reinterpreting it in the present.

In spite of references in the Gospels to something being the case, 'in order that Scripture might be fulfilled', it is clear that for Jesus the mere presence of something in Scripture does not mean that because God has spoken it cannot therefore be open to (re)interpretation. The Jewish tradition of engagement with Scripture that Jesus inherited, and that persists to this day, demands interpretation and reinterpretation precisely so that the will and call of God can be clearly known in the present. The fulfilment of Scripture for Jesus involves being open to God's call to listen, to learn, to discover something new. Almost every part of Scripture that Jesus himself quotes he expands, reinterprets, and applies in a fresh way to the present. In the company of Jesus opening Scripture leads to the invitation to take with full seriousness God's word received in the past; make clear conforming or contradictory connections with current experiences, hopes and fears; and discover what is God's living word for now.

Prescribed by the Bible

Confining what it means to 'be biblical' to knowing and following the laws of God as they are set out in the Scripture is limiting, excluding and potentially inappropriate, especially, as I showed in chapter 7, when this forms the approach taken by church leaders who claim a monopoly of knowing the mind of God. One way forward is to reject such over-tight text-bound ways of being biblical in favour of an approach that claims to follow 'biblical values' such as love, truth, faithfulness and mercy. It is then easy to reject 'laws of God' that appear in the Bible on the ground that they do not fit in with our own moral stances, so we think they no longer apply because what we really need to adopt is the 'spirit' of Scripture. It is important to discover the thrust of the teaching of Scripture, and how Scripture can speak to present day-situations that weren't thought of when the Bible was being written, using 'Scripture to interpret Scripture'. But for two reasons, the adoption of a general 'biblical values' approach is no real solution. First, choosing which 'scriptural values' to adopt can be as arbitrary as choosing which laws of Leviticus must apply in the present and which can be left in the past. Second, there is an inevitable tendency to decide which values are to be counted as godly or biblical by projecting the consensus of current social values back onto the Bible. In other words, the Bible is called upon to reflect the culture and aspirations of the reader rather than the other way round.

One way around this dilemma would be to reject the possibility of the Bible having anything to offer to present-day pastoral practice. But pastoral practitioners who claim to be Christian must be prepared to engage hospitably, critically and with real openness to the possibility of God speaking in the present through the words of Scripture. Being biblical does not mean turning occasionally to the Bible for help when we meet a puzzling pastoral situation. That would be like family members only speaking to each other when they want something to be handed over, but otherwise living in estrangement under the same roof. To be biblical is to live in a continuing, comfortable, and argumentative relationship with the Bible. It means living in the *oikonomia*, the household, where the speaking of God is expected to be experienced as part of everyday normality. The habit of listening to the Bible, speaking its words, singing its songs, dwelling on its pictures, reflecting on its teachings, allowing its messages to grate and bore as well as to comfort and stimulate, is the essential context for discovering what it means to include the speaking of God in pastoral practice. This makes for mature adult relationships with the Bible rather than childish ones which as we grow up have to be put away (1 Corinthians 13:11).

I have a friend called Bernard who is a Franciscan Friar. Each day he joins with his brothers for Morning Prayer, which consists mainly of sequential Bible readings and Psalms. They stop what they are doing for Midday Prayer – about 15 minutes of short Bible reading, Psalm, reflection and prayers. At Evening Prayer they continue their Bible readings and praying the Psalms. Before they sleep they come together for Night Prayer. At some point during the day they celebrate Holy Communion, which brings together readings from the Old and New Testament and from the Gospels. In between all this they work as cooks, gardeners, teachers, social workers, professors, circus clowns, pastors . . . Their whole life is both 'steeped in Scripture' and thoroughly practical.

To other Christians this might sound inspiring or ghastly. But such commitment to encounter with the Bible is not limited to clergy, monks and nuns. Many Christians frame their spirituality around regular engagement with the Bible alongside their practical commitments, using Scripture reading plans, Bible reading notes, etc. This regular 'practice of Scripture' serves to build up a sense of living by God's grace in continuity with the communities of the Bible. Edward Farley, writing of the formation of Christian pastors, speaks of the need to develop *habitus* and *theoria* – ways of living and ways of seeing that instinctively take account of God's presence and purposes in the world.[2] One way of putting this could be to describe someone as learning to 'speak Bible', just as people learn to speak English or Serbo-Croat or Japanese – by growing up in families where it is used every day. It should be obvious that I am not arguing for present-day Christians to fix their 'speaking Bible' in a particular tradition of discourse or interpretation, as (say) the Amish people of Pennsylvania have done in the past, but to recognise their daily lives in the context of a Bible that speaks the language of the present. This is much more likely to yield reliable identification of what is required by the word of God than the arbitrary selection of texts to justify 'must have' or 'must not do' or 'must be'.

Stepping into the Bible

The Bible contains very few long sections of theoretical explanation of what the stories in it actually mean. Even the big prophetic books of the Old Testament and the Epistles to the Romans and to the Hebrews, perhaps the most theoretical of New Testament texts, make more sense if they are seen as examples of responsive, contextual pastoral teaching, preaching and argument rather than free-standing theological monologues. Certainly, there are lots of pointers in the New Testament to the meanings of the events surrounding Jesus and the first Christians, but these most often take the forms of further stories or teaching about (say) what it might mean for Christians to see themselves as the 'body of Christ'.

The vast majority of the Bible takes the form of overlapping stories, prayers and sayings. Often the context and purpose of the stories is apparently clear (such as the story of David and Bathsheba in 2

Samuel 11:1ff); sometimes the context is much less clear, such as the stories of Job or Jonah or the background to the Book of Revelation. Practical engagement with the Bible involves listening carefully to a wide range of overlapping, sometimes repeated, often contradictory and confusing stories, and having stories of one's own to contribute. It means asking what kinds of stories they are and why they are being told at all. Traditional teaching about meditation can be very helpful here as it guides people to identify in turn with different characters in the stories, to hear their tones of voice as well as what they say, and to see themselves as part of the story and listen carefully for what God has to say.

At this point Bible scholars are likely to throw up their hands in horror, arguing that this kind of 'narrative theology' approach is doomed to failure because it only a thinly-disguised form of subjectivism that allows people to make the Bible mean what they want it to mean. Certainly this is one of the risks of this approach, which is why safeguards are needed. But I think that this is not only a risk worth taking, but one that must be taken by pastoral practitioners who regard what they are doing as designed to express the gospel by promoting the care and respect of people. The gospel comes first as stories to be told and heard, not as propositional truths calling for intellectual assent.

Consider, for example, how the Gospel of John continues after the opening few sentences. 'In the beginning was the Word' and the section that follows are among the most theoretical pieces of theology in the whole Bible, yet even these are designed to evoke the vivid pictures of creation at the beginning of Genesis. Then, within a few lines, 'the Word became flesh and dwelt among us', and just a few more lines after that the rest of John consists almost wholly of stories, sayings and prayers of Jesus. Somebody once commented that in Jesus the Word became flesh, but too many theologians keep trying to turn flesh back into words again. The point about bringing the Bible and the experiences of everyday into overlapping relationship so that they resonate with one another is that this approach follows the direction chosen by the Word who is God – that he became flesh and is allowed to stay flesh. It is in this overlap with the stories, sayings and protests of Scripture that the stories and protests of pastoral practice find their greatest potency as resources for change. Allowing the Bible its own humanity as we reflect upon our own humanity is a key starting point in enabling people to become human and biblical at the same time.

Not Just the Psalms

Most Christians are happy to hear in the Psalms the struggles and joys of faith that echo with their own experience. From the spiritual confidence of Psalm 1, the exhaustion of Psalm 22, the almost crushed hope of Psalm 42 and the despair, longing and violence of Psalm 137, to the triumphal praises of Psalms 148–150, picture after picture is generated with a vividness that helps people easily to latch on to their own pictures and stories. But this lively dynamic is present almost throughout the Bible as the devoted, passionate and confused people we meet there are allowed speak from their 'present' experience into today's experience. In this sense the Bible is historical text and contemporary text at the same time.

Again it is important to avoid the danger of collapsing into subjectivism. People can assume that because human nature does not change, the stories of the Bible are about the same kinds of people that we meet as neighbours, friends, enemies and acquaintances today. In some ways they are, but to assume this without careful critical thought is a serious mistake. The starting point should not be that the people in the Bible are just like the people of today, *but the exact opposite*. They lived in the Middle East, thousands of years ago, spoke different languages, had social customs that seem to us different, exotic, attractive or disgusting; and had ways of relating to God, their neighbours and the rest of the world that are miles away from the experience of most people in the West today. Two straightforward examples will suffice. First, they assumed that God was present, active and speaking whereas the commonest working assumption in the West is that God is absent or disengaged. Second, popular cultures of the West are dominated by the autonomy and freedom of the individual. Isolated individualism has little part in Scripture, except as sin. The wonder and potency of the Bible comes from people today hearing echoes and seeing reflections in it of their own experiences and concerns. To be human and biblical means to allowing Scripture its variety of familiar voices, but also its utter difference – what I called in chapter 1 its foreignness. It means avoiding an over-ready identification of the peoples of the Bible with our own kith and kin so that their stories are really only our own stories thinly disguised. When the differences and the resonances are both given their full weight, the bridges can be built that make credible connections between the Bible and pastoral practice possible

Fixed Speech or Free Speech?

The writer of Hebrews, whose whole argument is rooted in reinter-
pretations of Old Testament Scripture, declares, '. . . the word of God
is living and active, sharper than any two-edged sword, piercing until
it divides soul from spirit, joints from marrow; it is able to judge the
thoughts and intentions of the heart'(4:12). The context is loaded with
quotations which are assumed to convey the authority of God's own
speaking. But for this writer the 'word of God' is far more than the
hauling of texts of Scripture from the past into the present situation.
The word of God is best understood as God speaking into the present
moment. The words of Scripture and the realities of the present situation come together to create moments of disclosure that require
responses of decision, commitment, loyalty, joyful celebration and
further questions.

In other words, whether the messages of Scripture texts are crystal
clear or allusive and clouded, they do not *in themselves* fix the speaking of God as a static reality that is rooted in the past and can only
speak in limited ways in the present. This would be to confine the
freedom of God. The freedom of people to think, decide and speak
derives not from post-enlightenment respect for individual persons,
but from the freedom which is characteristic of God himself. Just as
people need freedom of thought and speech in order to form communities of freedom, God needs freedom of speech to make his will
and purposes known. Being genuinely biblical involves discovering
the directions and the limits within which that freedom can blossom.
Keith Ward argues that:

> The tragedy of fundamentalism is that it is so utterly unbibli-
> cal . . . a truly Bible-based faith would see that fallibility and
> diversity, development and poetic vision, are basic characteristics
> of the Bible. It testifies to the fallibility of human understanding
> of divine revelation and the many different human perspectives
> on divine revelation, even as it corrects that understanding and
> moves us to new images of the divine.[3]

Being human and biblical at the same time involves allowing living
Scripture to speak to living people. The hard questions pastoral practice asks here are about how best to help this to happen faithfully and
fruitfully.

What is Human?

At the beginning of this chapter I asked whether being 'biblical' was likely to make people narrower or bigger as persons. This is an important question for pastoral practice, because people who claim most loudly to be acting or preaching biblically often display characteristics of narrow-mindedness on moral issues and lack of humanity in their treatment of other people they disagree with.[4] Their encounters with the Bible, and refusal to enter into serious debate with Christians who hold different views from theirs, sometimes seem to make them smaller and less mature as persons. That smallness and immaturity can also be imposed onto others.

The question of what is human features in a whole range of philosophical, ethical, political and theological discussions. Often it is asked in relation to boundary issues about the beginning and the end of life. When does a fertilised egg become a human being with human rights? When does human life end in a person whose body remains alive, but whose brain has died? Is somebody in a persistent vegetative state to be regarded as fully human? When, if ever, can euthanasia be justified? What ought to be the freedoms and limits of genetic research and intervention? Related to these is a wide range of other questions – religious, cultural and medical. What is meant by 'personhood', 'self', 'human dignity', 'human rights' and many other terms?[5]

Behind this bewildering range of ethical issues and moral perspectives lies another range of questions about the quality of human life. Should we be striving to find what human perfection might look like? Would a cloned human being be genuinely human? What learning can emerge from the experiences of people who suffer or are vulnerable? What responsibilities do different generations and different ethnic groups have towards one another? How do bonds of family, ethnicity, love and loyalty affect conflict and co-operation between different groups of people?[6]

All these questions contribute to the agenda of twenty-first century Christian pastoral practice and they are certainly relevant to the question of whether we can be human and biblical at the same time. However, to keep our discussion focused we need to concentrate on some of the theology of what it means to be human. I will offer a theological sketch of five essentials of what it means to be human. These are calling, covenant, wisdom, reconciliation and maturity.

1. Called to Be Human

The creation stories in Genesis tell of God's creating humankind 'in his image, in the image of God he created them; male and female he created them' (Genesis 1:27); and of God forming 'the man from the dust of the ground and [breathing] into his nostrils the breath of life, and the man became a living being' (2:7). But this living being is incomplete until his 'helper' is provided to bring him to effective life and fruitfulness (2:21–24). These three factors are basic to any biblical notion of being human – made in the image of God; brought to life by the breathing of God; created for relationship.

Being made in the image of God involves openness and hiddenness, clarity and mystery. The 'image of God' reflects the character of God – personhood, freedom, love, truth, integrity, purposefulness, self-giving, creativity, fruitfulness, etc. One implication of this is that everything that makes for the diminishment of people – that is designed to make them more of a thing and less of a person, to over-restrict freedom, to mask love and truthfulness, undermine integrity, rob them of purpose, creativity, fruitfulness – is an assault on the image of God in that person. The picture of God breathing into the form that is made of dust is very powerful. This scene has been described as 'having all the intimacy of a kiss'. The point here is that people are human because of the creativity, the breathing, the calling of God.

Being formed in the image of God both clarifies and clouds what it means to be human. It clarifies it because it shows that the further people mask or mar the image of God within them the less likely they are to be as fully human as God intends them to be. But it also clouds what it means to be human because the 'image of God' does not carry with it the idea that God can be fully and clearly known. In the deepest sense the person of God is a 'mystery'. 'Mystery' in theological language means a reality that can only partly be discerned in the present and that will be completely revealed in the fullness of God's time. This idea of the partial hiddenness of God is illustrated well in Exodus 33. Here we are told that 'the Lord speaks to Moses face to face as a man speaks to his friend' (v. 11). But only a few verses later in the same passage when Moses asks God to show him his glory he is told, 'no one can see me and live' and Moses is covered by the hand of God until he has passed by (vv. 20–23).

It can be argued that all this changes when Jesus comes on the scene and discloses fully and finally who God is when, as John puts it, 'No one has ever seen God. It is God the only Son . . . who has made him known' (1:18). Paul makes this point to the Colossians: 'in him the whole fullness of Godhead dwells bodily' (2:9) and Hebrews describes Jesus as 'the exact reflection of God's glory' (1:3). Certainly, Christians believe that Jesus Christ is the fullest and the final self-expression of God, but even this does not take away the sense of mystery that surrounds Jesus. Paul's meditation on the depth of God's love expresses this vividly, 'For now, we see in a mirror dimly, but then we will see face to face. Now I know only in part; then I will know fully, even as I have been fully known' (1 Corinthians 13:12).

The practical implication of this theological 'mystery' that people are made in the image of God is that people can be deeply known and valued through relationships of various kinds, but that they will also remain a mystery both to others and to themselves until the time when they are 'fully known'. To be fully human is to be fully known in the biblical sense of being in full and open relationship with God. People are human because of the calling and the breathing of God. Job expresses this in poetic language when he says, 'If he should take back his spirit to himself, and gather to himself his breath, all flesh would perish together, and all mortals return to dust' (34:14–15).

The sense in which this humanity combines both clarity and mystery is profoundly important for the practice of Christian pastoral care and for Christian preaching and teaching. Among other things it means that taking part in discussions about the Bible and pastoral practice on topics that Christians disagree about will need to involve a measure of humility, caution, tentativeness and reverence if the issues are to be fully and charitably explored.

2. Covenant

The biblical notion of covenant is important for our discussion of being human and biblical. In the Bible, being called by God is never a merely interior or private spiritual experience. 'Human autonomy is not even on the horizon of the Old Testament witness.'[7] It has two inescapable practical aspects. The first is that the calling is to do something or to say something. The second is that it is the calling to do or say something in company with other people who are also receiving the call of God. In the Bible the call of God to people is always personal. It sometimes takes place in a quiet and personal context (such as the call of Mary), but it is never finally worked out purely privately. Abstract personal belief and 'private faith' are absolutely foreign to the Bible. From the call of the man and woman in the garden to 'be fruitful and multiply', to the calls of the patriarchs, judges, kings and prophets, the calling of God always comes in the context of the covenant community of the people of God, and very often through people who are on the margins of that community. The theological theme of covenant dominates the Old Testament and related, less specifically Jewish, images are frequent in the New Testament. Its key features are a calling from God, the requirement for holy living, the promise of blessing to those who comply, the warning of trouble for those who rebel and the offer of mercy and renewal for those who repent.

This calling always points forward and outwards, as the prophet's call to the returning exiles makes clear, 'I have given you as a covenant to the people, a light to the nations, to open the eyes that are blind, to bring the prisoners from the dungeon, from the prison those who sit in darkness' (Isaiah 42:6–7). The legal and ritual expressions of God's covenant relationship with his people are set out in Deuteronomy and Leviticus – see especially Leviticus 19. The tender and wounded love and longing of God are expressed most clearly in Hosea. The warnings to those who break the covenant are most vividly expressed in Amos. The place of the individual in relation to the renewed covenant community is shown most clearly in Jeremiah 31:31–34. The point for our purposes is that to be fully human in biblical terms is to belong within the covenant community of the people of God and participate in the mission of the people of God.

3. Wisdom

To be human in biblical terms involves being open to the indwelling of wisdom. This is not simply a quality some people develop as they grow older – a sort of advanced version of common sense. In the Bible 'Wisdom' is a much richer and deeper reality. Wisdom is often portrayed as feminine and her two key characteristics are that she is present and that she speaks. She calls attention to the presence and the purposes of God. Proverbs is the most obvious focus of the role of Wisdom in the Bible, but Job, Psalms, Ecclesiastes and Song of Songs are also part of the 'Wisdom Literature'. In Proverbs, 'Wisdom cries out in the street; in the squares she raises her voice . . .' (1:20). She is both present and elusive. Her message is the call to turn away from wicked and idle speaking and actions, hear the truth about God and about people, search out what it means to do what is right and find fulfilment in the purposes of God. Much of what Wisdom has to teach sounds rather earthy and hard bitten – for example in 17:1 and 25:24;

and the tone of her teaching tends to grate with a sense of over-righteousness. But that is to misunderstand her purpose, which is to make clear the contrast between a life lived in response to the love and truthfulness of God and a life lived only for self-gratification. Jesus' teaching with its emphasis on being doers and not just hearers of the word (Matthew 7: 21ff) draws deeply on the Wisdom tradition of the Old Testament. The connection between Wisdom and being human comes from the observation that the inspiration, the presence, the provocation of Wisdom reveals the disruptive presence of the reality that in the New Testament is witnessed to as the Holy Spirit. In biblical terms to be on the road to being human is to be increasingly accessible and responsively open to the Wisdom of God.

4. Forgiveness and Reconciliation

The Bible is full of people making mistakes, committing crimes, getting lost, doing each other down, turning away from God and becoming enemies. And this is just the covenant people of God! From the beginning the covenant community had to find ways of keeping itself and its people clean before God. In the early days this was sometimes achieved in the harshest of ways, as we see in the treatment of Achan and his family in Joshua 7:16–26, of which there may be echoes in the death of Ananias and Sapphira in Acts 5:1–11. If there could be no way back, or out, for those who had fallen or become lost, there could be no way forward for anybody. Both the person and the people around them were likely to suffer in some way. Forgiveness and reconciliation are core themes in the covenant renewal teaching of Isaiah 40—55 and Ezekiel 36—37. The Ezekiel text is of especially important relevance for our question of what it means to be human. The prophet describes the people who have fallen away from God's ways as having become polluted with uncleanness and having hearts of stone – incapable of responding to the calling of God so, 'A new heart I will give you, and a new spirit (breath) I will put within you; and I will remove from your body the heart of stone and give you a heart of flesh' (36:26). For Ezekiel, the only way back to being truly human according to God's version of what it means to be human is by God's gift of forgiveness, healing and renewal experienced in community.

The Gospels often describe the actions and teaching of Jesus in terms of reconciliation, forgiveness, healing and renewal. John's Gospel presents Jesus' resurrection appearance to his disciples in the upper room in terms reminiscent of the creation of humankind with an account of his breathing on the disciples and saying, 'Receive the

Holy Spirit . . .' and going on to commission them for works of forgiveness, reconciliation and warning (20:21–22). This is quickly followed in the longer ending by the reconciliation of Peter (21:9–19). The hiding of the disciples in the upper room and the hidden-ness of Peter within himself symbolise them having become much less fully human than when they were present with Jesus as witnesses of his words and acts. The breathing is intended to make them fully human again for the tasks that lie ahead. In their reconciliation with the risen Jesus their humanity is restored and their purpose renewed.

Paul uses the creation theme to emphasise the effects of forgiveness and reconciliation: 'So if anyone is in Christ he is a new creation: everything old has passed away; see, everything has become new!' (2 Corinthians 5:17). In Ephesians the believers are called to turn away from bitterness and be 'kind to one another, tender-hearted, forgiving one another, as God in Christ forgave you' (4:32). For the New Testament writers, being set free to be truly human means being open to offer and to receive renewal, forgiveness and reconciliation both from God and from the people of God.

Basic to this whole notion of reconciliation is the need for repentance – the renewing of one's mind, the transformation of one's way of thinking. In Christian spirituality repentance has become closely linked with the action of penitence and the confession of particular sins. But the primary Christian confession is not, 'I've just shot my granny', or some other sin, but 'Jesus Christ is Lord'. In other words, repentance is about identity – who you are now that you have set out to follow Christ in the world, rather than just an owning up to what you have done. Paul captures this in Romans 12:1–3 as he draws the contrast between being compressed into the patterns of this world and being transformed by the renewal of your mind. Christian pastoral practice is intended to help people to become truly human by living in such a way that forgiveness, reconciliation and the transformations that come through the renewal of the mind become practical possibilities, not just religious fantasies. Commitment to the search for forgiveness and reconciliation are absolutely basic to discovering what it means to be human and biblical at the same time.

5. Maturity

'Maturity' can sound utterly boring – humourless, middle-aged, overweight, sensible, dull. It brings out in me a desire to play and rebel to discover where I can find joyfulness, fun, a different angle on things. Becoming fully human in response to God's call involves growing into maturity, but it does not mean becoming stagnant, formulaic and ossified in the way we handle the Bible. Jesus' words about receiving the kingdom of God as a little child suggest that God's people need to grow up and be childlike at the same time. The mature innocence, spontaneity, presupposition of trust, freedom to explore, wonder at discovery, openness to learn and readiness to protest of the child needs to be refreshed and renewed among the conventionalised adults who dominate the biblical gate-keeping leadership of the churches. Paul connects Christian growing into maturity with growing deeper in the love of God: 'When I was a child, I spoke like a child, I reasoned like a child; when I became an adult, I put an end to childish ways' (1 Corinthians 13:11).

Often people who claim to be biblical Christians are using criteria that are far from mature. These are rooted in careful study of the inspiration of the Holy Spirit in the past, and are committed to the readiness of the Holy Spirit to speak in the present, but they expect that the consistency of God's speaking demands that the same thing is always said and done now as was said and done then. God is holy and truthful, so the argument goes, therefore God's speaking in the present cannot be different from God's speaking in the past. I have already referred to this as the difference between free speech and fixed speaking. It implies, arguably, that God's original speaking was virtually context-free – that it came from completely outside of the peoples of the Bible and was intended to fix the practices, relationships, moral attitudes and actions of the people of God for all time. But this cannot be right, because as the transition from the Old Testament to the New Testament shows, there is room for a new speaking of God into new contexts in ways that come near, but not all the way, to re-expressing the whole agenda of God's purposes for God's people. So, in the New Testament, much of the Mosaic law is regarded as fulfilled, or set aside or re-prioritised; the role of sacrifice is completely re-interpreted in terms of the cross of Christ; the covenant community is redefined in terms of the body of Christ and the household of faith, and includes uncircumcised Gentiles.

It is arguable that if the speaking of God into the communities of the Bible is context-free, or even context-fixed, then it is not seriously relational or purposeful speech at all. Being human and biblical at the same time involves having sufficient maturity among local and global Christian communities to be able to attend to the tensions and differences, as well as the resonances and similarities that are essential features of the Bible being accepted as the foundational speaking of God across the boundaries of time, cultures and nations. People will be human and biblical when they bring deep humility, attentiveness, lightness of touch, a sense of fun, graciousness and critical questioning to their engagement with the Bible and pastoral practice.

The foundations of Christian maturity are well reflected in the prayer of Ephesians 3:14–21. This calls for the people to be 'strengthened in your inner being by the Holy Spirit'; having 'Christ dwell in your hearts through faith'; being 'rooted and grounded in love'; having power to comprehend, with all the saints (with all the communities of God's people, past as well as present) the full dimensions of things at the same time as knowing 'the love of Christ that surpasses knowledge'. The purpose of all this is 'that you may be filled with all the fullness of God'. Here the paradox of knowledge, and therefore a complete break with the inevitability of the link between knowledge and control, is expressed beautifully – to know the love that is fundamentally unknowable. It is unknowable in the sense that it cannot be possessed, restricted, confined or used by the knower as a source of power to restrict the freedom of God or of the people of God.

A little later in the letter (4:13), in the context of a reflection on the unity of God's people and the gifts of God, the writer refers to maturity directly. '. . . until all of us come to the unity of the faith and of the knowledge of the Son of God, to maturity, to the measure of the full stature of Christ'. This refers not just to individuals coming to maturity, but to 'all of us'. The people of God are called to move towards a corporate maturity that perhaps allows for different people to grow at different rates, but that has as its standard measure, 'the full stature of Christ'. This is clearly an eschatological reference rather than an immediate prospect that will be completed cheaply or quickly. There is a poster in the office where I work that shows a puppy of the Chinese fighting dog – the Shar Pei – which is covered with a deeply wrinkled skin. The caption underneath says, 'God isn't finished with me yet!' Maturity involves accepting the present reality and living in the light of the future hope. The Shar Pei dog will always be a Shar Pei, but the maturing Christian will grow into the likeness of Christ. As Bonhoeffer and other theologians have observed, the people of God are called to be fully human, even as Jesus Christ is fully human. I have heard this taken further by the theological reflection that I will only be fully me when you are allowed to be fully you.[8] This in itself should generate a certain humility and reverence in the way Christians seek to be human and biblical at the same time. Premature closure of what it means to be biblical may indicate a failure to recognise what is involved in the call to become fully human.

Who Are 'We?'

In the question of whether we can be human and biblical at the same time it matters a lot who 'we' are. I propose therefore that the 'we' of the question are people who are historical, local and global. 'We' are historical because we are inheritors and extenders of the tradition of Bible interpretation. We are local because we cannot but encounter Scripture in the contexts in which we live. We are global because each local church is part of the whole church.

'We' Belong Within History Not Outside of It

I have already explored some of the meanings of tradition for interpreting the Bible in chapters 1 and 2, so I will limit the discussion here to reflection on two key words that are associated in Christian theology with the notion of taking part in history. These are tradition and remembrance – in Greek *paradosis* and *anamnesis*.

Tradition

Paradosis carries the sense of receiving and passing on something that has been entrusted to you. Its range of meanings includes gift, trust and risk. Passing on the 'traditions of the fathers' expresses this well. Unlike conservationists who want to preserve things from risk of further change, the expectation is that each generation will receive the Christian tradition, examine it with care, make it their own, contribute to it and pass it on, so that while it keeps its fundamental integrity, it is constantly being renewed. 'Tradition' is something that develops and changes through time. That is why the appeal to tradition cannot in itself be sufficient justification for attitudes of defensive conservatism towards changes in public worship, or of pastoral practice. Because tradition is a living reality, not simply a repetition of the past, it has to be allowed its voice so that it can play its part in teaching, questioning and inspiring Christian pastoral practice in the present.

In Protestant theology it has been the convention to draw a distinction between the inheritance of Scripture as the Word of God and the 'man-made' traditions of the Church. There are good reasons for this, but there is also a danger because *the Bible is part of the tradition of the Church*. This is important because if we are to think of the 'Great Tradition' as living and developing it is essential to have confidence in the foundations it is building upon. If the tradition of the Church is to be recovered from lapsing into a rehearsal of the discoveries, inspirations, sins and misguided-ness of the past it is vital to recognise that the Bible and the continuing life of the people of God belong together. This does not take away from the priority of the Bible, but it does place the Bible within the life of the Church, not outside of it.

Passing on something as precious and holy as the Bible is clearly a major commitment to trusting that generations to come will handle the tradition faithfully and make their contribution with integrity as they pass it on. Tradition is a gift from the past to the future through the filter of the present. But handing on the tradition is also an enormous risk precisely because it never remains unchanged and is always at its best subject to re-appraisal. Parts of the tradition can get screened out by the filters of particular generations and interest groups and have to be rediscovered and reintegrated later on – such as the virtual disappearance of women from the annals of Christian history except in stylised roles as nuns, saints, queens and mothers. Just as God's speaking is never context-free, neither is present-day engagement with tradition. Tradition is received as gift, trust and risk as the witness to how in Christian worship, practice and mission God's people have sought or neglected to be biblical and human at the same time.

Remembrance

Anamnesis – the Greek work for remembrance – means far more than recollecting as a series of facts the things that happened yesterday. It carries the meaning of remembering something important that happened in the past, and that took place long before you were born, but with two special perspectives. These are that you remember *as if you were there* and that *the action of remembering brings into the present the effects of what happened in the past*. A simple example in Britain is Remembrance Day – 11 November – when the nation remembers with gratitude the sacrifice of those who served in the First Word War, which ended at the 11th hour on the 11th day of the 11th month of 1918, and in all the wars involving Britain since then. At the heart of Holy Communion, for many Christians the most important action in worship, lies the call to remembrance: 'Jesus said, "Do this in remembrance of me."' The notion of this kind of remembrance is absolutely central to what it might mean to be biblical and human at the same time. The whole purpose of Scripture is that God's people may remember the foundational gift of God's word spoken 'to our ancestors in many and various ways by the prophets, but in these last days . . . by a Son . . .' (Hebrews 1:1–2).

When Christians read Scripture they are called to open up their imagination and their critical faculties to fresh breathings of the Holy Spirit so that they hear and read the Bible as if they were there and in the expectation that this remembering of Scripture has the potential to make a difference in the present. These two aspects of remembrance are closely linked to a third. The regular practice of the remembrance of Scripture and the remembrance of the words and actions of Jesus has major implications for the spiritual formation of Christian believers. The imaginative act of faith that I have described as remembrance leads to *re-membering* – the joining back together of the people of God, who under the pressures of life tend to drift apart from God and from one another.

Finally, 'remembrance' also carries a potential for discomfort and protest. The fact is that I was *not* there at the time when the war was fought and ended. I was *not* there when Jesus first broke the bread on the night that he was betrayed. So I have to face up to another question. Since I was not there then, and since this is all supposed to be so important, what is it all supposed to mean here and now? In other words, the actions of remembrance and of actively engaging with the gifts, trusts and risks of tradition have two dynamics that depend for their continuing liveliness on each other. First, they are about accepting the radical connectedness of Christians today with the people of the Bible. Second, they are about accepting the radical disconnectedness between Christians today and the people of the Bible. Without the first, claims of Christian experience and commitment today become less and less connected with a faith that has its roots in Scripture and its growth in the inheritance, for good and ill, of Christian tradition. Without the critical questioning of the second, the tradition and the remembrance soon lose any claim on the present and will regress into becoming 'just history'. To be human and biblical at the same time involves living with the discomfort and the protest that arise from the connections and the disconnections that come from taking part in the living tradition and the active remembrance of the speaking and actions of God.

Local and Global

Throughout Scripture God's call is experienced personally and locally, but its reach goes far beyond the merely local. The call of Abram contains the assurance of God's protection and the promise that 'in you all the families of the earth shall be blessed' (Genesis 12:3). Second Isaiah's message to the exiles begins with the assurance of God's comfort and forgiveness, but moves straight on to the expansive vision that 'the glory of the Lord shall be revealed, and all people shall see it together' (40:5). Matthew's Gospel ends with Jesus sending his followers 'to make disciples of all nations' (Matthew 28:19). Luke's second book opens with the risen Christ 'commissioning' his disciples to be witnesses to him 'in Jerusalem, in all Judea and Samaria, and to the ends of the earth' (Acts 1:8); the Bible begins and ends with the connection between the speaking of God and the gift of the light of God's glory for all the earth. But this vision is quite beyond the reach of many of God's people. God's people then, as now, seem to have an inexorably tendency to take what God intends for everybody, shape it to fit their own culture, and privatise it for their own use.

To be human is to be formed by the localities that we belong to, though this is never a simple picture because most people belong to a whole number of overlapping localities in different aspects of their lives such as their home setting, their workplace and their leisure activities. People also belong to a whole range of localities of the imagination that they inhabit almost without realising it – TV soaps, the cyber-communities of internet chat rooms, special interest communications networks. Whatever our localities, we will tend to see things from where we are and then generalise values, principles and preferred courses of action from that point of view. The universal becomes a projection of the local.

This is reasonably uncomplicated if you are able to stay with the post-enlightenment modernist perspective in which the global is simply a much bigger version of the local. The laws of science and nature are basically the same out there as they are in here. Human desires are basically the same everywhere and so are human needs. God's call to the people in one part of the world will be basically the same as his call to people anywhere else. To be sure, the similarities may be hard to discern because they may be masked by the overlay of local culture and different value systems. But since truth is absolute and universal, what is true in one place will be true everywhere. Christian values and practices in one place will be just as recognisable as proper Christian values in another. In terms of Christian mission and pastoral practice this means that when you get the message clear, all you need to do is to ensure that everybody everywhere believes the same kinds of things in the same kinds of ways so that the salvation of Christ is spread across the whole world.

But there are problems with the assumption that the global is a bigger version of the local. This 'top down' version of what is held to be true enough to form the biblical basis for pastoral practice simply does not always work. Increasingly people and groups in different parts of the world, or even within the same communities, are claiming a hearing for what is 'true for me even if it is not true for you'. This post-modern demand that truth, even biblical truth, can mean different things in different places lies at the heart of much conflict within churches about what beliefs and practices can be guaranteed to be authentically Christian. Official attempts to find agreement between Christians taking different sides on issues like same-sex relationships, the theological legitimacy of free-market capitalism, the rights of the unborn child, intercommunion between Roman Catholics and other Christians, etc. on the basis of intellectual and confessional assent to agreed propositional truths can clear some ground, but in themselves do not get people very far. This is partly because that kind of approach is almost inevitably elitist, leaving behind the vast majority of ordinary believers who find it irrelevant to the pressing demands of daily living.

Story Sharing

Is there, then, no hope of being both biblical and human in a post-modern world where the local and the global are no longer totally separate but come so close together that they frequently overlap? This is where the strategy of witnessing to the speaking and action of God by the use of stories can have real mileage. John Drane draws on the work of Carl E. Amerding, who highlights six advantages of hearing the Bible as story.[9] These are:

1. It takes account of all scholarly methods, but is not exclusively bound to any of them.
2. It does not prejudge the possible meanings of Scripture, for it honours the text as it is, rather than dismantling it.
3. Stories leave open questions related to the spiritual and the supernatural.
4. Because they focus on the whole spectrum of human experience, stories speak directly to our life concerns as we encounter them existentially moment by moment.
5. It is incredibly easy for stories to cross cultural boundaries.
6. Stories invite participation.

Through the shared experience of telling, hearing, questioning, respecting and re-telling, stories can become catalysts for the creation of communities that can accommodate difference as the same time as being open to renewal. The careful sharing of story can bring to the surface the core values that different people can contribute towards the decisions and actions of pastoral practice.

This emphasis on being biblical and human at the same time through the sharing of biblical and contemporary story will be seen as deeply unsatisfactory by people who want to stake claims for the priority of Scripture over experience. Indeed, I have great sympathy with such criticism. However, there is a further step we need to take before rejecting this approach as necessarily leading Christian pastoral practice away from Scripture rather than towards it.

I said earlier that each of the slippery words in the question must be separated so that we could explore the issues. Now we need to bring them back together. We have seen that being biblical and human at the same time cannot mean a simple loosening-up of present-day attitudes towards the practices and beliefs that are witnessed to in Scripture. That is, it cannot mean a simple loosening of the connection between the word of God in Scripture and the word of God among Christian believers in the twenty-first century. Neither can it mean projecting the social consensus of the present backwards onto the Bible, nor an uncritical and uncurious hauling of Scripture texts from the past into the present. For Christian pastoral practice to be biblical and human at the same time demands heightened attention to what kind of thing the Bible is; to what it means to be truly human through the breathing of God; and to what it means to live in radical connectedness with the communities of the people of God in *both* the past and the present. The resources provided by seeing Scripture primarily in terms of story have the potential of encouraging strong and creative connections between the agendas and realities of pastoral practice and of Scripture. Among the stories that are told and shared by Christian pastoral practitioners the story of the Bible has priority because it is the first and foundational story of Christian faith – the story from whose perspective all other human stories are to be told and heard, evaluated, renewed and acted out. The hard questions pastoral practice asks of the Bible are all about what it means to be human and biblical at the same time.

Notes

Chapter 1: What Is a Bible?

1. *The Concise Oxford Dictionary*, ninth edition (Oxford: OUP, 1995).
2. David C. Steinmetz, 'The Superiority of Pre-Critical Exegesis' in Stephen E. Fowl (ed.), *The Theological Interpretation of Scripture* (Oxford: Blackwell, 1997), p. 29.
3. Ibid., p. 28.
4. AV; 'the law was our disciplinarian until Christ came', NRSV.
5. Of course, we need to recognise that the Canon of the Old Testament was still not fixed by the first century CE, and that the range of texts regarded then as 'Scripture' or 'almost Scripture' was wider than the present Canon.
6. A highly critical brief survey is in Walter Brueggemann, *Theology of the Old Testament* (Minneapolis: Fortress Press, 1997), pp. 1–56. For a good readable brief survey of types of New Testament criticism see Raymond E. Brown, *An Introduction to the New Testament* (New York: Doubleday, 1996), pp. 20–47.
7. For the view that Calvin rejected the conclusions of Copernicus's study, see Bernard Cottret, *Calvin* (Edinburgh: T. & T. Clark, 2000), pp. 285–6; for a contrary view, see Alister E. McGrath, *Christian Theology: An Introduction* (Oxford: Blackwell, 1994), pp. 141–3.
8. An entertaining discussion of the results and limitations of historical-critical approaches to the Bible is provided in John A. T. Robinson, *Can We Trust the New Testament?* (London: Mowbray, 1977). See especially pp. 30–44.
9. John Goldingay, *Models for Interpretation of Scripture* (Grand Rapids: Eerdmans, 1995) pp. 128–9.
10. Richard A. Burridge, *What Are the Gospels? A Comparison with Graeco-Roman Biography* (Cambridge: CUP, 1992).
11. For an accessible discussion of the positive role of critical biblical studies see James Dunn, 'The Bible and Scholarship: On Bridging the Gap between the Academy and the Church', *Anvil*, vol. 19, no. 2, 2002, pp. 109–18.
12. Anthony C. Thiselton, *The First Epistle to the Corinthians: The New International Greek Testament Commentary* (Grand Rapids: Eerdmans, 2000).
13. Brueggemann, *Theology of the Old Testament*, 1997.
14. Christopher Rowland, *Christian Origins* (London: SPCK, 1985), pp. 3, 296f.
15. For a useful summary article on the formation of the Canon see Bruce M. Metzger and Michael D. Coogan (eds), *The Oxford Companion to the Bible* (Oxford: OUP, 1993), pp. 98–104.
16. Rowan Williams, *Open to Judgement* (London: DLT, 1994), p. 160.
17. C. F. D. Moule, *Forgiveness and Reconciliation: Biblical and Theological Essays* (London: SPCK, 1998), p. 214.

18. This point still applies in spite of the fact that there are variations of opinion between major churches about which books are to be regarded as canonical, as is seen in the Roman Catholic Church's acceptance of the Apocrypha.

19. For a very readable account of the Reformation's struggles to get the Bible translated into English see David Daniel, *William Tyndale, A Biography* (New Haven: Yale University Press, 1994).

Chapter 2: How Does the Bible Relate to the Word of God?

1. See e.g. Matthew 23:23–24.

2. F. W. Bourne, *Billy Bray: the King's Son* (London: Epworth Press, 1937).

3. Timothy Ward, 'The Bible, Its Truth and How It Works' in Paul Gardner and Chris Green, *Fanning the Flame: Bible, Cross and Mission* (Grand Rapids: Zondervan, 2003), pp. 17–41.

4. Ibid., my italics.

5. Stephen E. Fowl, *Engaging Scripture* (Oxford: Blackwell, 1998), pp. 120–27.

6. Ibid., p. 125.

7. The relevant wording of Article VI reads '. . . so that whatsoever is not read therein, nor may be proved thereby, is not to be required of any man, that it should be believed as an article of the Faith, or be thought requisite or necessary to salvation'.

8. Justin Martyr, *Apology* in Cyril C. Richardson (tr. and ed.), *Early Christian Fathers* (London: SCM, 1953), p. 270.

9. Stephen I. Wright, 'The Bible as Sacrament', *Anvil*, vol. 19, no. 2, 2002, p. 81.

10. A sacrament is 'an outward and visible sign of an inward and spiritual grace', *A Catechism: Book of Common Prayer*, 1662.

11. Wright, 'The Bible as Sacrament', p. 83, italics original.

12. Matthew 8:27, Mark 4:41, Luke 8:25.

13. Olivier Clément, *The Roots of Christian Mysticism* (London: New City, seventh edition, 2002), p. 53–54.

14. Dan Hardy, correspondence quoted in Archbishops' Council, *Formation for Ministry within a Learning Church*, (London, Church House Publishing, 2003), p. 42.

Chapter 3: Who Owns the Bible?

1. A major initiative in bringing members of different faith groups together to consider their Scriptures is provided by Michael Ipgrave (ed.), *Scriptures in Dialogue: Christians and Muslims Studying the Bible and the Qur'an Together* (London: Church House Publishing, 2004).

2. G. R. Evans, 'The Middle Ages to the Reformation' in John Rogerson (ed.), *The Oxford Illustrated History of the Bible* (Oxford: OUP, 2001), p. 191.

3. David Wright, 'The Reformation to 1700' in Rogerson, *The Oxford Illustrated History of the Bible*, pp. 200ff.

4. Lamin Sanneh, *Encountering the West: Christianity and the Global Cultural Process: The African Dimension* (London: Marshall Pickering, 1993), p. 7.

5. Lamin Sanneh, *Translating the Message: The Missionary Impact on Culture* (Maryknoll NY: Orbis Books, 1999), p. 1ff.

6. James J. Stamoolis, *Eastern Orthodox Mission Theology Today* (Maryknoll, NY: Orbis Books, 1986), p. 26f. quoted by Sanneh, *Encountering the West*, p. 82 (my italics)

7. Dr and Mrs Howard Taylor, *Biography of James Hudson Taylor*, (London: China Inland Mission/Overseas Missionary Fellowship, 1965), pp. 78ff. (Hudson Taylor arrived in China in 1854.)

8. Vincent J. Donovan, *Christianity Rediscovered: An Epistle from the Masai* (Indiana: Fides/Caretian, 1978). See, for example, pp. 28ff. For a major discussion of understandings of Christian mission during the post-Enlightenment period see David J. Bosch, *Transforming Mission: Paradigm Shifts in Theology of Mission* (Maryknoll NY: Orbis Books, 1993), pp. 262ff.

9. Vincent L. Wimbush, 'The Bible and African Americans: An Outline of an Interpretive History' in Stephen E. Fowl (ed.), *The Theological Interpretation of Scripture* (Oxford: Blackwell, 1997), pp. 70–86.

10. Ibid., p. 71.

11. Ibid.

12. Ibid., p. 74.

13. Ibid.

14. Ibid., p. 79.

15. Desmond Tutu, *The Rainbow People of God: South Africa's Victory over Apartheid* (London: Transworld, 1994), pp. 143–152.

16. Ibid., p. 81.

17. I recognise that this begs the questions of which sections of the Bible can be regarded as mythological and of what status myth should be allowed to have in relation to the revelation of truth.

18. Kathleen Fischer, *Women at the Well: Feminist Perspectives on Spiritual Direction* (London: SPCK, 1989), p. 93.

19. Ibid.

20. Phyllis Trible, *Texts of Terror: Literary-Feminist Readings of Biblical Narratives* (London: SCM, 1992).

21. Ibid., p. 28.

22. Ibid., p. 36.

23. Ibid., p. 64.

24. Ibid., p. 92.

25. Rosemary Radford Reuther, *Women and Redemption: A Theological History* (London: SCM, 1998), see especially pp. 30–8.

26. Daphne Hampson, *After Christianity*, (London: SCM, 1996/2002), see especially chapters II and IV.

27. Jenny Richardson, 'Reading the Bible in the City', *Anvil*, vol. 20, no. 2, 2003, p. 115.

Chapter 4: How Does the Bible Witness to Jesus Christ?

1. Two major and readable works that provide good starting points and comprehensive surveys are: Gerd Theissen and Annette Merz, *The Historical Jesus: A Comprehensive Guide* (London: SCM, 1998); N. T. Wright, *Jesus and the Victory of God*, vol. 2 (London: SPCK, 1996).

2. By 'the Gospels as they are presented' I mean the texts that are presented in the English Versions. In spite of the many variant readings and the plethora of translations, I think the stories, sayings, narratives and given reflections the New Testament Gospels contain (as distinct from the hermeneutical challenges they offer) are remarkably stable.

3. David Lyall, *Integrity of Pastoral Care* (London: SPCK, 2001), p. 106 (italics mine).

4. Jürgen Moltmann, *Theology of Hope* (London: SCM, 1967), see especially pp. 23ff.

5. Mel Gibson, *The Passion of the Christ*, Newmarket Films, 2004.

Chapter 5: Do Jesus and Pastoral Practice Belong Together?

1. Accessible introductions to these issues are: Joanna and Alister E. McGrath, *The Dilemma of Self Esteem* (Wheaton, Illinois: Crossway, 1992), see especially chapter 2; Heather Ward, *The Gift of Self* (London: DLT, 1990), see especially chapter 2; Alastair McFadyen, *The Call to Personhood: A Christian Theory of the Individual in Social Relationships* (Cambridge: CUP, 1990), for a more thoroughgoing treatment.

2. See Stephen Pattison, *Shame: Theory, Therapy, Theology* (Cambridge: CUP, 2000). See especially pp. 154ff. for a full discussion.

3. Sam Keen, *To a Dancing God* (London: Fontana, 1970), p. 142, quoted by Kenneth Leech in *Spirituality and Pastoral Care* (London: Sheldon Press, 1986), p. 38.

4. Leech, *Spirituality and Pastoral Care*. p. 38.

5. David Brown *Tradition and Imagination: Revelation and Change* (Oxford: OUP, 1999), p. 278.

6. Ibid.

7. David Brown, *Discipleship and Imagination: Christian Tradition and Truth* (Oxford: OUP, 2000).

. Ibid., p. 209.

9. Alastair V. Campbell, 'Pastoral Care' in Wesley Carr (ed.) *The New Dictionary of Pastoral Studies* (London: SPCK, 2002), p. 252.

Chapter 6: Is the Bible a Bridge or a Boundary?

1. BBC News Words Edition report, 23 July 2004, www.bbc.co.uk/2//europ

2. Articles of Religion, *Book of Common Prayer*, 1662.

3. See for example the discussion about the primary importance of 'value' in Keith Ward, *A Vision to Pursue* (London: SCM, 1991), pp. 178–92.

Chapter 7: Where in the Church Does the Bible Belong?

1. Stephen Fowl, *Engaging Scripture* (Oxford: Blackwell, 1998), pp. 26–7.

2. Ibid., p. 89.

3. Grace Davie, *Religion in Britain Since 1945: Believing without Belonging* (Oxford: Blackwell, 1997).

4. It is no coincidence, for example, that the birth and resurrection narratives

in Matthew and Luke include stories of visits by strangers, which emphasise the new world that is opening up as a result of an encounter with
Christ. The Bible is full of such visitation narratives which often take place
in the context of hospitality.

5. Two seminal studies, the first historical, the second theological, would serve
as foundational texts for this wide-ranging topic: Perez Zagorin, *How the
Idea of Religious Toleration Came to the West*, (Princeton: Princeton University
Press, 2003), see especially pp. 14–45; Miroslav Volf, *Exclusion and Embrace:
A Theological Exploration of Identity, Otherness and Reconciliation* (Nashville:
Abingdon Press, 1996), see especially pp. 193–231.

6. An important and eminently readable study of toleration is: Jonathan Sacks,
The Dignity of Difference: How to Avoid the Clash of Civilisations (London:
Continuum, 2002), see especially pp. 105ff.

7. Keith Ward, *What The Bible Really Teaches: A Challenge for Fundamentalists*
(London: SPCK, 2004), pp. 90–1.

8. Ibid., pp. 18–28.

9. Ibid., p. 23.

10. Ibid., p. 81.

Chapter 8: Can We Be Human and Biblical at the Same Time?

1. Ezekiel 34.

2. Edward Farley, *Theoria: The Fragmentation and Unity of Theological Education*
(Philadelphia: Fortress Press, 1983).

3. Keith Ward, *What the Bible Really Teaches*.

4. A useful exploration related to this field is Lawrence Osborn and Andrew
Walker, *Harmful Religion: An Exploration of Religious Abuse* (London: SPCK,
1997).

5. A useful theological starting point for this exploration is Alistair Y.
McFadyen, *The Call to Personhood* (Cambridge: CUP, 1990). A compelling
narrative/reflective approach is provided by Frances Young, *Face to Face: A
Narrative Essay in Theology and Suffering* (Edinburgh: T. & T. Clark, 1990).

6. A helpful inter-disciplinary survey of such issues is provided by *Being
Human: Readings from the President's Council on Bioethics* (Washington DC:
The President's Council on Bioethics, 2003).

7. Walter Brueggemann, *Theology of the Old Testament: Testimony, Dispute,
Advocacy* (Minneapolis: Fortress Press, 1997), p. 450.

8. Desmond Tutu, Sermon at Franciscan Third Order Conference, University
of York, August 1999.

9. Carl E. Amerding, 'Faith and Story in Old Testament Study: Story Exegesis'
in Philip E. Satterthwaite and David F. Wright, *A Pathway into the Holy
Scripture* (Grand Rapids: Eerdmans, 1994), pp. 31–49, quoted in John Drane,
The McDonaldization of the Church (London: DLT, 2000), pp. 141–3.

Bibliography

Abraham, William J., *Canon and Criterion in Christian Theology* (Oxford: OUP, 1998).

Archbishops' Council, *Formation for Ministry within a Learning Church* (London: Church House Publishing, 2003).

Ballard, Paul and Holmes, Stephen R., *The Bible in Pastoral Practice: Readings in the Place and Function of Scripture in the Church* (London: DLT, 2005).

Bosch, David J., *Transforming Mission: Paradigm Shifts in Theology of Mission* (Maryknoll NY: Orbis Books, 1993).

Bourne, F. W., *Billy Bray: the King's Son* (London: Epworth Press, 1937).

Brown, David, *Tradition and Imagination: Revelation and Change* (Oxford: OUP, 1999).

—*Discipleship and Imagination: Christian Tradition and Truth* (Oxford: OUP, 2000).

Brueggemann, Walter, *Theology of the Old Testament: Testimony, Dispute, Advocacy* (Minneapolis: Fortress Press, 1997).

Burridge, Richard A., *What Are the Gospels? A Comparison with Graeco-Roman Biography* (Cambridge: CUP, 1992).

Carr, Wesley (ed.), *The New Dictionary of Pastoral Studies* (London: SPCK, 2002).

Clément, Olivier, *The Roots of Christian Mysticism* (London: New City, seventh edition, 2002).

Cottret, Bernard, *Calvin* (Edinburgh: T. & T. Clark, 2000).

Daniel, David, *William Tyndale: A Biography* (New Haven: Yale University Press, 1994).

Donovan, Vincent J., *Christianity Rediscovered: An Epistle from the Masai* (Indiana: Fides/Caretian, 1978).

Drane, John, *The Mcdonaldization of the Church* (London: DLT, 2000).

Farley, Edward, *Theologia: The Fragmentation and Unity of Theological Education* (Philadelphia: Fortress Press, 1983).

Fischer, Kathleen, *Women at the Well: Feminist Perspectives on Spiritual Direction* (London: SPCK, 1989).

Fowl, Stephen E., *Engaging Scripture* (Oxford: Blackwell, 1998).

— (ed.), *The Theological Interpretation of Scripture* (Oxford: Blackwell, 1997).

Gardner, Paul and Green, Chris, *Fanning the Flame: Bible, Cross and Mission* (Grand Rapids: Zondervan, 2003).

Goldingay, John, *Models for Interpretation of Scripture* (Grand Rapids: Eerdmans, 1995).

Hampson, Daphne, *After Christianity* (London: SCM, 1996/2002).

Ipgrave, Michael (ed.), *Scriptures in Dialogue: Christians and Muslims Studying the Bible and the Qur'an Together* (London: Church House Publishing, 2004).

Leech, Kenneth, *Spirituality and Pastoral Care* (London: Sheldon Press, 1986).

Lyall, David, *Integrity of Pastoral Care* (London: SPCK, 2001).

McFadyen, Alastair, *The Call to Personhood: A Christian Theory of the Individual in Social Relationships* (Cambridge: CUP, 1990).

McGrath, Alister E., *Christian Theology: An Introduction* (Oxford: Blackwell, 1994).

McGrath, Joanna and Alister E., *The Dilemma of Self Esteem* (Wheaton, Illinois: Crossway, 1992).

Metzger, Bruce M. and Coogan, Michael D., *The Oxford Companion to the Bible* (Oxford: OUP, 1993).

Moltmann, Jürgen, *Theology of Hope* (London: SCM, 1967).

Moule, C. F. D., *Forgiveness and Reconciliation: Biblical and Theological Essays* (London: SPCK, 1998).

Osborn, Lawrence and Walker, Andrew, *Harmful Religion: An Exploration of Religious Abuse* (London: SPCK, 1997).

Pattison, Stephen, *Shame: Theory, Therapy, Theology* (Cambridge: CUP, 2000).

Radford Reuther, Rosemary, *Women and Redemption: A Theological History* (London: SCM, 1998).

Richardson, Cyril C. (tr. And ed.), *Early Christian Fathers* (London: SCM, 1953).

Robinson, John A. T., *Can We Trust the New Testament?* (London: Mowbray, 1977).

Rogerson, John (ed.), *The Oxford Illustrated History of the Bible* (Oxford: OUP, 2001).

Rowland, Christopher, *Christian Origins* (London: SPCK, 1985).

Sacks, Jonathan, *The Dignity of Difference: How to Avoid the Clash of Civilisations* (London: Continuum, 2002).

Sanneh, Lamin, *Encountering the West: Christianity and the Global Cultural Process: The African Dimension* (London: Marshall Pickering, 1993).

—*Translating the Message: The Missionary Impact on Culture* (Maryknoll NY: Orbis Books, 1986).

Taylor, Dr and Mrs Howard, *Biography of James Hudson Taylor* (London: China Inland Mission/Overseas Missionary Fellowship, 1965).

Theissen, Gerd and Merz, Annette, *The Historical Jesus: A Comprehensive Guide* (London: SCM, 1998).

Thiselton, Anthony C., *The First Epistle to the Corinthians: The New International Greek Testament Commentary* (Grand Rapids: Eerdmans, 2000).

Trible, Phyllis, *Texts of Terror: Literary-Feminist Readings of Biblical Narratives* (London: SCM, 1992).

Tutu, Desmond, *The Rainbow People of God: South Africa's Victory over Apartheid* (London: Transworld Publishers, 1994).

Volf, Miroslav, *Exclusion and Embrace: A Theological Exploration of Identity, Otherness and Reconciliation* (Nashville: Abingdon Press, 1996).

Ward, Heather, *The Gift of Self* (London: DLT, 1990).

Ward, Keith, *A Vision to Pursue* (London: SCM, 1991).

—*What the Bible Really Teaches: A Challenge for Fundamentalists* (London: SPCK, 2004).

Williams, Dick and Shaw, Frank, *The Scouse Gospel* (London: White Lion Publishers, 1967).

Williams, Rowan, *Open to Judgement* (London: DLT, 1994).

Wright, N. T., *Jesus and the Victory of God* (London: SPCK, 1996).

Young, Frances, *Face to Face: A Narrative Essay in Theology and Suffering* (Edinburgh: T. & T. Clark, 1990).

Zagorin, Perez, *How the Idea of Religious Toleration Came to the West* (Princeton: Princeton University Press, 2003).

Index